The
CLIMBER'S
H A N D B O O K

The
CLIMBER'S
HANDBOOK

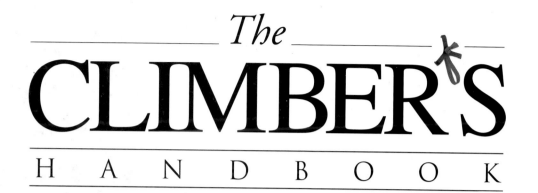

Garth Hattingh

First published in 1998 by
New Holland (Publishers) Ltd
London · Cape Town · Sydney · Singapore

24 Nutford Place
London W1H 6DQ
United Kingdom

80 McKenzie Street
Cape Town 8001
South Africa

3/2 Aquatic Drive
Frenchs Forest, NSW 2086
Australia

ISBN 1 85368 717 0

Senior Designer: **Trinity Fry**
Editors: **Anouska Good** and **Simon Pooley**
Publishing Manager: **Mariëlle Renssen**
Illustrators: **Annette Busse,**
Steven Felmore and **Chip Snaddon**
International Consultant: **Jon Tinker**
Australian Consultant: **Greg Mortimer**

Reproduction by Unifoto (Pty) Ltd
Printed and bound in Singapore
by Tien Wah Press (Pte) Ltd

AUTHOR'S ACKNOWLEDGEMENTS

I would like to thank Keith, my colleague and mentor, for many pleasurable times spent in the mountains, for instilling a regard for safety to temper my rashness, and for helping to instigate my involvement with training. I would also like to thank all of the many friends and pupils who climbed with me over the years and who have helped to make the mountains a special place of beauty and adventure. Thanks to Martin who helped create and proofread a good deal of the material, under difficult conditions, and lastly to the long-suffering editors and designer, Anouska, Simon and Trinity, for their tactful help and inspiring professionalism.

The mountains are the means, the man is the end.
The idea is to improve the man, not to reach the
top of mountains. Climbing only makes sense if
you consider the man.

Walter Bonatti, *On the Heights*

FOREWORD

The most important discovery of my life, some forty-five years ago, was that of climbing. I love it, am obsessed by it, as much now as on that first day when a friend of the family took me to Harrison's Rocks, a little sandstone outcrop to the south of London. That day I discovered an activity for which I had a natural ability and which seemed to have a limitless capacity for personal discovery. I was still at a day school in London, but from that moment on I took every available opportunity to hitchhike out for holidays in Snowdonia and Scotland, working my way up the climbing grades, discovering the joys of mountaineering on the Isle of Skye, the challenge of winter climbing in Scotland, then reaching out to the wider horizons of the Alps and then the Himalayas.

Over this period I have seen an extraordinary development and expansion of this sport, which is so much more than a sport. It is an obsession, a way of life, a joy, a growing and ever-widening sense of awareness. I started with a pair of clinker nailed boots, a second-hand hemp rope and a couple of nylon loops with ex-WD carabiners. The top standard in the early Fifties was around E1. Joe Brown and Don Whillans had just started their climbing campaign that was to revolutionize British rock climbing, but to me they were just a distant rumour – though I started repeating their routes in 1953, in some instances making second ascents. It's easy to be nostalgic, but they were great days. There were not many people around, and climbing was wonderfully simple – it didn't pay to fall off when you were leading with only a couple of runners which usually comprised slings draped over convenient flakes or threaded around stones jammed in cracks.

Yet today, I use all the latest devices – Quickdraws, RPs, Rocks, Walnuts, Friends, chalk – and this has enabled me to keep up a fairly high standard of climbing, E2 5c on a good day, at a reasonable level of risk. I hate to think of the long falls I boldly risked, as we all had to, in my youth. And yes, I go to the indoor climbing walls and do a bit of sport climbing, which I find fun – but I believe passionately that it should be kept off the traditional crags. Bolt-protected climbing is a pale imitation of the real thing, for it is the presence of risk that is the fundamental basis of the attraction of climbing. Once a crag has been covered in bolts not only has man, or for that matter, woman, imposed their presence on the natural environment, but they have removed that fundamental challenge of accepting the natural protection that the rock offers.

So what do I get out of climbing? A lot more than 'because it's there'. It is very similar to what Garth Hattingh describes here in *The Climber's Handbook*: it starts with the physical satisfaction of clambering up a stretch of rock, essentially the satisfaction of an athlete; but where climbing starts being different and so much stronger an experience, is that element of risk, that you are staking your life on your judgement. There is the sense of discovery, both of your own limits and of places where no-one has ever been before. There is the wonder of the beauty of the mountains, the strength of friendships, when your life is literally in your climbing partner's hands. Certainly there's competition, even in traditional climbing. The sense of achievement of being the first to solve a boulder problem, of snatching a new route from under the noses of your peers, of being the first to top out on an unclimbed peak. The secret of staying alive and going on enjoying the mountains is finding a balance in all these motives for climbing.

I hope this beautifully illustrated book will help you discover for yourself the joy of climbing.

Chris Bonnington

CONTENTS

BROOKS RANGE

ALASKA RANGE

ROCKY MOUNTAINS

SIERRA
NEVADA

APPALACHIAN
MOUNTAINS

ATLANTIC

OCEAN

PACIFIC

OCEAN

GRAMPIANS

PYRENEES

ATLAS
MOUNTAINS

ANDES

ANDES

ANDES

ANDES

BRAZILIAN
HIGHLANDS

KEY TO MAJOR CLIMBING AREAS OF THE WORLD

Sport climbing

Traditional climbing

Snow and ice climbing

Alpinism

Aid and big wall climbing

Super-alpinism and expeditions

TJEN MOUNTAINS

URAL MOUNTAINS

STANOVOY
RANGE

SAYAN MOUNTAINS

ALPS

CAUCASUS

TIEN SHAN

JAPANESE ALPS

ZAGROS
MOUNTAINS

KARAKORUM

HIMALAYAS

ETHIOPIAN
HIGHLANDS

INDIAN

OCEAN

MACDONNELL
RANGES

DRAKENSBERG

GREAT
DIVIDING RANGE

SOUTHERN
ALPS

SOUTHERN   OCEAN

CHAPTER ONE

INTRODUCTION
The Essence of Climbing

Climbing is gaining rapidly in popularity, with the *International Sports Yearbook* of 1996 rating it as one of the fastest growing sports in the world. The reasons for this are as diverse as the various climbing disciplines for, after all, 'climbing' can vary from unencumbered solo scrambling up a sunny, head-high boulder to freezing for days and nights on an 8000m (26,250ft) peak as part of a 20-person international expedition.

Why climb? George Mallory's motive for climbing Everest – 'Because it's there' – during the British expeditions of the 1920s is certainly one reason, while curiosity about what is 'on the top' (or other side) has served as a spur to climbers for centuries. The ascetic stimulus of a challenge, to test one's courage, or to make a personal statement, are also all valid and frequently stated motives.

One of the (often unrecognized) major reasons is the 'focusing of attention' that the sport demands. As one approaches one's limits in climbing, the field of attention – vision, sound and touch – narrows to a tiny cone. The cares of the world are displaced by tightly honed concentration. As one climber put it:

Early oxygen equipment.

'If I was a laser, I would have burned that rock clear through!' This escape from everyday reality to a heightened sense of awareness – with its slow, continuous adrenaline burn and surges of panic, joy or activity – is frequently the true motivator of climbing. Any rock climber will recognize this, just as any walker who has been lost in mist

A climber savours the challenge amid the scenic beauty of Garden of the Gods, Colorado, USA.

will acknowledge the drowning out of all but the essential moment, and the strange sadness experienced on returning to the harsh realities of daily life.

When approached correctly, with appropriate skills and equipment, climbing is not as dangerous as many people think. Improved equipment and procedures have rendered once hazardous routes relatively safe, and many climbs which were the 'desperate firsts' of the past are now done as a fun outing by parties of average skill and experience. Today's extreme challenge often turns out to be tomorrow's mild adventure, but this is not to denigrate the efforts of the earlier pioneers – it is always far more difficult to be the 'first' at anything.

Tenzing on the summit of Everest, 29 May 1953.

REINHOLD MESSNER

Reinhold Messner started climbing at the age of five and climbed extensively in his teens with his brother in the Italian South Tyrol. At 20 he climbed the Walker Spur on the Grandes Jorasses, Mont Blanc Range, held by many to be the most beautiful route in the world because of its length, committing nature, exposure, and elegant situation.

In 1975 he and his long-term climbing partner, Peter Habeler, knocked off the Eiger North Wall in an amazing 10 hours – and went on to perform the first true alpine-style climb on an 8000m peak when they ascended Gasherbrum I (8068m; 26,470ft) in the Karakorum. Messner went on to ascend virtually every significant large mountain in the world, including solo ascents of Nanga Parbat (Himalayas) and the North Face Route of Everest. He made the first oxygenless ascent of Everest, with Peter Habeler in May 1978, and was the first man to climb all 14 of the 8000m peaks. An articulate and outspoken person, Messner is one of the 'gurus' of mountaineering.

That said, it should however never be thought that mountaineering can ever be risk-free. The famous alpinist, Paul Preuss, wrote:

'We know only too well that fate can turn you from winners into losers. Only people who don't grasp this will treat their own life lightly. People who clearly understand that this is the nature of the game, and even say so, should not be demeaned.'

This is sadly as true for the sea-cliff top-rope scrambler as for the Everest summiteer. The nature of adventure activities is such that some form of accident may occur, no matter how carefully one guards against it. In fact 'risk' is often given as one of the major factors in the popularity of climbing. Not that mountaineers are, or ever should be, unnecessary risk-takers.

Reinhold Messner, one of the world's greatest mountaineers, who has repeatedly stated that his first priority in mountains is 'to deliver constantly [his] own life from the claws of death,' says:

'Fun and reality, success and failure, life and death keep close company, as do heat and cold, sunshine and storm, rock and ice. It is not heroic to launch oneself into borderline situations regardless of the consequences. In mountaineering a hero does not live long; to know no fear can mean perhaps not coming back.'

Striving to be safe without spoiling the challenge or the enjoyment is probably the ultimate goal of every climber. It is to this end that this book is written – to encourage people to take to the rocks, hills and mountains, but to help them do so with suitable knowledge, skills, and the right mental approach. There is a lot of useful information not only for the beginner but also for the more experienced climber.

As a beginner, if safety is high on your list (and it should be), then beware of going it alone. Join up with competent climbers, sign on for a climbing course, find a local club and take part in its activities. Simply reading this handbook will not equip you to zip safely up a small rock climb, let alone head for K2 as expedition leader! The old adage holds true: 'There is no substitute for experience'.

THE FOURTEEN 8000+ METRE PEAKS

PEAK	HEIGHT (M)	1ST ASCENT	EXPEDITION
Everest	8848	1953	British
K2	8611	1954	Italian
Kangchenjunga	8585	1955	British
Lhotse	8516	1956	Swiss
Makalu	8463	1955	French
Cho Oyu	8201	1954	Austrian
Dhaulagiri	8167	1960	Swiss
Manaslu	8163	1956	Japanese
Nanga Parbat	8125	1953	German
Annapurna	8078	1950	French
Gasherbrum I	8068	1958	USA
Broad Peak	8047	1957	Austrian
Shisha Pangma	8046	1964	Chinese
Gasherbrum II	8035	1956	Austrian

NOTABLE ASCENTS

Mont Blanc (France)	4807m (15,771ft)	M. Paccard, J. Balmat	1786
Matterhorn (Switzerland)	4478m (14,692ft)	Whymper, Croz, Douglas, Hudson, Hadow, Taugwalder	1865
Kilimanjaro (Tanzania)	5895m (19,341ft)	H. Meyer, L. Purtscheller	1889
Mount Kenya (Kenya)	5199m (17,058ft)	H. Mackinder	1889
Aconcagua (Argentina)	6959m (22,832ft)	E. Zurbriggen	1897
Illimani (Bolivia)	6462m (21,202ft)	M. Conway, A. Maquignaz, A. Escobar	1898
McKinley (Alaska)	6194m (20,322ft)	H. Stuck, R. Tatum, W. Harper	1913
Logan (Canada)	6050m (19,850ft)	American–Canadian expedition	1925
Peak of Communism (Russia)	7485m (24,558ft)	E. Abalakov	1933
Annapurna (Nepal)	8078m (26,504ft)	M. Herzog, L. Lachenal	1950
Nanga Parbat (Pakistan)	8125m (26,658ft)	H. Buhl	1953
Everest (Nepal)	8848m (29,030ft)	E. Hillary, N. Tenzing	1953
K2 (Pakistan)	8611m (28,252ft)	L. Lacedelli, A. Compagnoni	1954

A BRIEF HISTORY OF MOUNTAINEERING

Mountains, with their aura of mysticism and adventure, have always fascinated humankind. They can be places of solitude – or the arena for great achievements.

From the earliest accounts, one finds mountains associated with the great religions of humanity, and with philosophers, artists, sages and scientists. Many peaks are still believed to be sacred, with the actual summits being off limits, for instance the Himalayan peaks of Kangchenjunga, 8585m (28,167ft); Machapuchare, 6993m (22,944ft); and Kailas, 6700m (21,982ft), which is held to be the Throne of Shiva and is the centre of Hindu and Buddhist worship. Native North Americans still regard desert spires as ancestral holy places and a 'no-go' to climbers. This mystical-religious theme echoes throughout the world – Mount Olympus, the home of the Greek Gods; Mount Kenya, the place of spirits for the Kikuyu; Mount Sinai and

Climbers skirt a crevasse on Everest, 1953.

the Ten Commandments. The high places are often linked to the great and noble thoughts of humankind.

This book is more concerned with the adventure side of climbing, although the exploits of the adventurers, thinkers, artists and mystics are inextricably woven into the fabric of mountaineering as a sport. People's reactions to mountains have undergone distinct changes through the years, from the very early age of superstition (in 1690 the Bishop of Geneva undertook a 'journey of mortal peril' to exorcize the glaciers of Chamonix, which as 'the worke of the deville were crushinge the barns'), via the great era of romanticism and exploration to the present time, which is sometimes cynically called the 'age of exploitation'.

It is perhaps hard for us to imagine the kind of superstitious fear with which our ancestors regarded these inaccessible peaks, believed to be inhabited by spirits, demons, and monsters of every form. Yet the Tibetan and other mountain people still today hold very similar beliefs.

Any history of climbing will inevitably do great disservice to the many unsung pioneers of countless centuries – one cannot doubt that Mount Olympus, the home of Greek mythology, was 'first ascended' at some stage – and the same goes for multitudes of other peaks and mountain passes. However, records of ascents were not kept, and the mountain historian can only go on that which is written.

The Western world would probably credit the first ascent of Mont Blanc (in 1786) by the local Chamonix climbers, Michel Paccard (a scientist) and Jacques Balmat (a crystal hunter), as the birth of 'true moutaineering'. The supposedly impregnable Jungfrau was ascended by the Swiss Meyer brothers in 1821. The time between the formation of the first mountaineering club, the Alpine Club, in 1857 and the epic disaster on the Matterhorn, the famous Whymper saga of 1865 (*see* panel), is referred to as the Golden Age of Alpine mountaineering. During this period, over 200 great peaks of Europe were climbed, largely by British mountaineers with their Alpine guides.

Indeed it was only when mountaineering became a popular pastime for the British gentry of the late nineteenth century that the 'sport' was truly born. The Alpine Club, with its sprinkling of judges, professors and clergy, gave the activity instant respectability but, for many years, 'scientific studies' were used as an increasingly thinly veiled excuse for mountaineering.

MAESTRI'S BOLT LADDER

Cerro Torre - a slender, storm-lashed, ice-plastered tower (3133m; 10,279ft) in southern Patagonia - is still regarded as one of the more challenging spires.

In 1959 Cesare Maestri, a renowned Italian climber, claimed a heavily contested first attempt from the northeast along with Toni Egger. Egger was killed in a violent storm during their descent and Maestri could subsequently recall little detail of the climb or the summit, leading to doubts as to whether they had ever in fact summitted.

In 1968 a British team attempted the climb from the southeast, but were repulsed near the summit. Maestri then repeated the British route and claimed a second ascent. To succeed, however, he had placed a 'bolt ladder' up the top pitches using a compressor-driven drill.

A storm of protest followed this, particularly after a party doing the route the following year bypassed most of the bolts using free-climbing techniques. The peak was finally ascended in classic, bolt-free style in 1974 by an Italian party.

Sherpas have always provided invaluable service to Himalayan expeditions.

Soon significant ascents were being made of already climbed peaks by new and more difficult routes – climbing was being done for climbing's sake alone. The Guggi route on the Jungfrau by Rev. George; the Brenva Ridge of Mont Blanc by the British climbers Adolphus Moore, Horace and Frederic Walker (father and son), George Mathews and the local guides Melchior and Jakob Anderegg; and the numerous bold and imaginative routes of Britain's Albert Mummery, were the first great 'variation' routes. The Europeans were represented by true mountaineers such as France's Michel Croz and Switzerland's Alexander Burgener, the precursors of today's highly skilled Alpine guides who still pioneer new routes every season. Even a pope, Achille Ratti (later Pope Pius XI), took part on a new route on Mont Blanc, the Grises route, just before becoming pontiff. Marie Paradis, a French villager, was the first female to ascend Mont Blanc in 1808; women were increasingly being drawn to the peaks.

The allure of climbing spread around the world. The American Rev. William Coolidge climbed 600 'grand courses' (a term then used to describe one of the recognized Alpine routes, comprising the ascent of an individual, separate summit) with his aunt and his dog, while the Swiss Lochmatter brothers – Franz and Joseph – also made their presence felt. The 1900s saw a phenomenal amount of climbing until World War I interrupted things, with outstanding new routes by climbers such as Humphrey Jones; Geoffrey Winthrop-Young; Armand, Georges and Jean Charlet; George Mallory; Laurent Croux; Jules and Maurice Simond; and Winthrop-Young's companion and guide, Josef Knubel. Climbs were taking place in Britain, America, Australia, South Africa, New Zealand, and South America.

In America, Colorado had already been identified as a great area, the focus of American climbing. Here, the Rocky Mountains sweep suddenly upwards out of the plains, a great tidal wave of geological upheaval, offering a full range of rock climbing from bouldering to alpine-style ascents and big wall routes. The concept of climbing more difficult routes 'just for the heck of it' began to emerge, and the Boulder area, encompassing Hallet's Peak, Estes Peak, and Long's Peak (called 'The American Matterhorn' with its steep and unforgiving East Face), became one of the focal points of effort.

The European Alps were still considered to be the real proving ground, however, and the opening (or 'first') ascents evoke the heroic feats of great climbers from many countries. Certain names stand out, such as Italy's Riccardo Cassin for his amazing ascent of the notoriously treacherous Walker Spur of the Grandes Jorasses in 1938; the first ascent of the Eigerwand (North Face of the Eiger) by the German-Austrian team of Anderl Heckmair, Ludwig Vörg, Heinrich Harrer and Fritz Kasparek in the same year; and in 1955, Walter Bonatti's solo ascent of the Dru in six days.

In 1954 two British greats, Don Whillans and the incredible Joe Brown, hit the Alps with a vengeance, achieving several notable firsts. The British climbers Chris Bonington, Ian Clough, Don Whillans and Jan Djoglosz's made a successful attempt on the Central Pillar of Freney in the Mont Blanc massif in 1961.

The Americans, too, stormed the European Alps in the mid-'60s, and climbers such as John Harlin, Gary Hemming and Royal Robbins went on to pioneer outstanding routes such as the American Direct on the Dru.

In America, local climbers began to tackle the peaks of Boulder, Colorado, as well as the walls of the Yosemite Valley. These challenges forced up climbing standards and attracted climbers from around the world, all eager to prove themselves on the test pieces of the day. Routes with evocative names such as The Naked Edge are still held in awe today because of their limited protection and technical difficulty.

As the playgrounds of Europe and America succumbed to the onslaught of increasing numbers, the leading climbers started to turn to some of the other grand mountain ranges of the world. Eyes were fixed for many years on the 8000m (26,250ft) peaks, and of course, prime amongst them, Everest. By the early 1900s, the British in particular, with their Imperial connections with India, had started to spiral in on Chomolungma, the Mother Goddess of Mountains (as Everest is called by the Chinese), but it was not until 1953 that Edmund Hillary and Sherpa Tenzing finally stood on the summit.

Thereafter, expedition after expedition to the Himalayas followed, until all of the 8000m peaks had been climbed. Then the variation routes began, with the Himalayas recently being referred to as the 'super Alps'. Oxygenless ascents, one-day alpine-style pushes, winter routes, and harder and harder variants are now a part of the Himalayan game, with faster and more daring attempts of necessity replacing new-routing.

In the 1970s and '80s, South America, in particular Patagonia, Southern Chile and Argentina, attracted the 'hard men', and the easily accessible peaks of Bolivia and of Peru drew the rest. Many new, bold lines were made, including the Italian Cesare Maestri's controversial 'bolt ladder' up Cerro Torre, in southern Patagonia (*see* panel opposite).

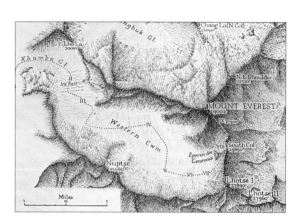

Some modern 'targets' include the frozen and windswept mountains of Patagonia, Antarctica and the Canadian hinterland. Their remoteness and the difficulty of access make these worthy challenges indeed for today's adventurer and it will probably be many decades before every peak has seen an ascent. It is somehow comforting to know that, for the pioneering climber, there are still many goals.

The history of modern climbing cannot, however, be disassociated from advances in equipment. One can hardly compare the primitive tribesman, standing in his bearskins and sandal-wrapped feet and quaking in awe of the looming summits, with the modern Goretex-swaddled climber in his plastic boots and crampons. Ropes, protection equipment, clothing, footwear, camping and survival gear have all undergone a radical revolution in the past quarter of a century. While this has made certain aspects of climbing easier, those seeking challenges have turned to harder and more demanding routes, have repeated routes in winter conditions, or in other ways 'raised the handicap'.

For above all else, climbing is no more than a game, one with rules and ethics, handicaps and etiquette. The consequences of 'bad play' might be more serious than in other sports, but it is nonetheless a game, a diversion, a hobby, a sport.

This early (1953) map of the Everest region is surprisingly accurate – considering the limited surveys which had been possible.

Whether on mountains or dam walls, climbers will find a way to practise their sport.

PLAYING BY THE RULES

To ascend a rock face solo and naked is probably the purest form of the art, although there is a fair chance that the climber trying this will be arrested and deposited in a lunatic asylum! Climbing with equipment starts to alter the chances of success or survival. To ascend a normal, easy, alpine rock route using fixed ropes, ladders, drilled bolts and protection equipment makes the whole exercise ludicrous; for a pair of climbers to do the same route using standard climbing gear places the exercise within 'acceptable rules of play'. An element of uncertainty in the outcome of any climb is the ultimate goal of the true adventure climber, and the rules are set to match the situation in order to allow this to happen.

To some extent, the mountain must have a chance! Lito Tejada-Flores, in his landmark essay *Games Climbers Play*, equated climbing to a set of games. A climber may select smaller stakes with a short, easy sport route that makes no real demands – or may choose to go for a gamble of monumental proportions, such as pioneering a new route, solo, in winter, on K2.

The 'game' of climbing differs from many sports in that it has flexible rules which alter according to the nature of the challenge and the ambition and abilities of the party. Generally, the more extreme the challenge, the fewer the rules – they are simply not necessary as the mountain sets its own rules, the breaking of which can lead to disaster.

The simpler and less extreme the 'game', the more 'rules' have to be instituted to make success in the activity a true achievement. In fact, the only discipline of climbing which has absolutely fixed and written 'rules of play' is the new arrival on the scene, competition climbing.

Let us examine some of the disciplines:

COMPETITION CLIMBING

Here the challenge takes place on artificial surfaces, where the ascent of routes of graded difficulty has to be completed in a specified style in a specified time. This is a popular option, with many devotees and immediate public appeal. Believed to be one of the fastest growing sports in the world, it is also the safest form of climbing, with little chance of serious accident (although the odd belaying error or carabiner failure has led to severe injuries). Major world competitions at present include the European-based World Cup circuit, invitation competitions such as Cerre Chevalier in France, Arco in Italy, and the Extreme Games in the USA. The growth in the junior section has been exponential, with major regional and international competitions, including both Youth (under 13) and Junior (under 19) World Cup series, currently being held annually.

Competitions fall under the CICE (Comité Internationale des Competitions d'Escalade) which is a subcommittee of the powerful UIAA (Union Internationale des Associations d'Alpinisme), the body which regulates and monitors world climbing.

INDOOR WALL CLIMBING

Although these walls or 'rock gyms' started out largely as training venues for natural rock climbing and later for competitions, the proliferation of indoor walls has led to a new branch of the sport, and some climbers never leave the 'plastic', as it is known. Here again the sport can have very restrictive rules, such as 'climb only on the yellow holds' or 'not past that line'. It is easily accessible, requires little equipment or experience, and is an excellent way to get started. As an end in itself it is highly satisfying, with immediate and frequent rewards and a great social aspect. There are walls in most major centres, but the greatest numbers are to be found in countries such as Belgium, the UK and the USA.

As with the next two disciplines, the major danger in wall climbing is tendon or muscle injury. Beginners should start gradually, building up the necessary power and strength (*see* page 70 for useful hints).

Indoor walls are rapidly growing in popularity, and offer excellent training venues without weather restrictions.

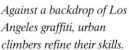

Against a backdrop of Los Angeles graffiti, urban climbers refine their skills.

Right Bouldering is one of the more sociable forms of climbing.

Below Thailand's tufas (drip-stone formations) are perfect for bouldering.

Right Soloing allows great freedom but is not without risk.

BOULDERING

As one gets out into the natural arena, bouldering appears to be the simplest option – you climb a low piece of rock to the top, you jump off if you can't make it, you try again until you do. However, many rules, unwritten but pervasive in the climbing community, govern its practice: you cannot use points of aid, you cannot use a rope from above, in some areas the use of chalk is frowned on, you are not allowed help from your partner, and so on. 'Boulders' can vary from half a metre (1.6ft) to a frightening 10 or so metres (33ft) high.

Bouldering had its origins in Fontainebleau, in France, where scaling the vast numbers of perfect sandstone boulders in the former royal hunting forest became a pastime for French climbers such as Jacky Godoffe, a prime exponent of this art.

The tools for bouldering are a chalk bag – usually filled with light magnesium carbonate or one of the numerous commercial variations – to dry your fingers and improve your grip, and a pair of sticky-rubber climbing boots. This is a good cheap entry level to the sport of rock climbing.

For many, bouldering is an all-consuming passion, with winters being devoted to hours in the 'cellar' (the climber's own small, indoor training facility), and drier days being given over to thousands of repetitions of a sequence of moves on desperately steep but short overhangs until the problem is 'cracked'. It is a highly gymnastic activity, demanding tremendous finger strength and power; almost invisible edges and awkwardly-angled moves are the order of the day. Bouldering has its own grading system (*see* grade table on page 152).

Variations on the bouldering theme are:

Free Solo Climbing

This involves 'bouldering' on anything from normal boulder height to huge rock faces where to fall could mean, and has brought about, certain injury or death. There are world-renowned exponents of this, such as John Bachar of America, but many top climbers solo to some extent at some stage.

If all goes well on the day, and both the nature of the route and the physical and mental state of the climber are excellent, then it is a pure form of the climbing art. It is not to be undertaken lightly, however, as a good number of superb climbers have ended their careers and often their lives in the pursuit of this rather deadly game.

Deep Water Soloing

In areas such as the Calanque in the south of France, and parts of the British coast, long spectacular traverses or climbs can be found. To fall from the cliffs means a wetting, sometimes a long swim, and embarrassment, but seldom anything more. The attraction of climbing unfettered by ropes or any other equipment draws many to this, particularly on a warm summer's day. Perhaps a manufacturer will soon create the perfect waterproof chalk bag!

Above, left and bottom
Deep water soloing is safe –
as long as you can swim!
Some committing routes
do, however, take one danger-
ously high above the water.

TOP-ROPING

This game allows for generally safe and exciting climbing up to considerable heights with little, if any, risk as the rope is fastened to solid, 'bombproof' anchor points at the top of the climb.

It is frequently the way to start beginners, but many climbers choose it as their usual or only form of climbing. It should not be disparaged, as it can be highly demanding physically and caters for the climber who likes his excitement but has absolutely no form of death wish! In many areas, such as the sandstone cliffs south of London or the American desert sandstone, it is the only permissible way to climb, apart from soloing.

In the famous Verdon Gorge in France, climbers top-rope the vast limestone cliffs on ropes as long as 300m (985ft). Should the climber come adrift lower down, rope stretch guarantees him a 30 to 40m (100 to 130ft) fall before he is held, often many metres out from the overhanging cliffs! A team of sweating climbers hoisting a companion back up through space is not an uncommon sight.

The rules of top-roping can be stringent – no 'tight rope' (support on the rope), no pulling on slings or other points of aid, no resting on the route, and so on; or they can be relaxed, as in a fun outing for friends or family.

SPORT CLIMBING

In climbing terms, this is also a modern game. It has its roots in the Alpine areas of France, where guides started to fix pitons (*see* page 72) into valley areas to allow for the efficient guiding and teaching of clients. The advent of battery-powered drills and the development of high-tech epoxy resins has led to increasing numbers of rock areas being 'bolted'. Holes are drilled into the rock along a suitable climbing line, and bolts are either glued in or tightened, with 'hangers' – suitable for clipping carabiners into – fastened to the protruding end (*see* page 73).

However, bolting is a controversial topic in many areas of the world, and can become a major issue in the granting of access to climbing areas. It is often considered to be a defilement of the natural rock, and has led to many heated debates. On the other hand, there are certain types of rock where bolts are the only reliable means of protection, e.g. certain limestone and granite crags. Climbers can lead up steep, usually overhanging routes in safety, clipping their rope into these bolts as they climb past.

Sport climbing has led to the rising standards of extreme rock climbing, with climbers able to push their physical limits without undue risk. These skills do transfer onto longer alpine or natural-gear routes, and there is little doubt that some of the modern extreme climbs in the mountain ranges of the world stem directly from the techniques and fitness derived from sport climbing. As an end in itself, sport climbing is challenging, demanding and immensely satisfying. In reality, it is 'high level bouldering', requiring the same gymnastic approach and dedication at the cutting edge of the sport. It has also provided safe, accessible climbing to many thousands of people who would, for various reasons, never get involved with natural-gear leading.

NATURAL-GEAR ROCK CLIMBING

This is what most people conceive climbing to be – one person 'leads' up a rock climb, trailing the rope and placing various pieces of rock climbing protection or 'gear' in cracks and fissures to protect herself or her followers should she fall. It is the traditional way to climb and still the most common.

Often called 'traditional' or 'trad' leading, it is also referred to as 'adventure climbing' and has a wide variety of rules, depending on the arena in which it is played. Trad climbing can range from small crags up to Alpine and Himalayan rock spires. To place a piece of gear and pull or stand on it on a small local crag is 'unacceptable', to do the same on the last pitch of the Trango Tower in the Himalayas after a five-day storm-filled ascent would probably be considered 'acceptable'.

Trad climbing can be further subdivided:

Crag Climbing

Crag climbing is practised on smaller outcrops, from 20 to 100m (65 to 330ft) in height, with only a few 'pitches' of climbing. The aim is to climb them 'free', that is, without resorting to any artificial aid. It is the most popular discipline in the UK, areas of Europe, the USA, and countries like South Africa and Australia.

Continuous Rock Climbing

This is 'super cragging' and takes place on longer multi-pitch climbs, where the crags are longer than 100m (330ft) or so, such as parts of the USA, and the European Dolomites. Equipment may be used for direct aid, e.g. pulling on a sling. The main rule is a one-day time limit.

Big Wall Climbing

The objective is to get the whole team up a large rock face such as El Capitan in the Yosemite Valley, or a Dolomite face, by 'fair means or foul'. The nature of the climb is such that aid may well have to be used, i.e. climbers could either place new pieces of gear, or use existing ones.

Only one team member is required to climb each pitch, with the followers usually jumaring or prusiking (*see* page 92) up the ropes behind the leader, thus saving both time and energy. Hauling sacks of food and equipment, and overnight bivouacs on the wall are par for the course.

The boundaries between these sub-games are now becoming increasingly blurred as techniques and equipment improve. For instance, many big walls are now being climbed 'free' (without aid).

ETHICS AND MOUNTAINEERING

The ethics of climbing are, by and large, determined by consensus within the climbing community - often by a slow process of osmosis - and can vary greatly from situation to situation. Visiting areas without being aware of this can lead to problems; for example, the ban on protection placements on the sandstone towers of Slovakia or Bowles Rocks near London, or the fact that when climbing in Fontainebleu, France, chalk is frowned on - 'poff', a resin, is used instead.

Doing a climb within the accepted set of rules means doing it 'in style'; doing it using the wrong rules is 'bad form' or even 'unethical'.

Climbers can generally be counted on to respect normal conservation and other social ethics, such as restrictions because of bird-nesting seasons or religious convictions. However, they are also notorious for shooting down 'sacred cows', for instance the necessity for over-elaborate permits or being landed with exorbitant advance 'rescue fees' in some national parks.

Do remember that your actions as a climber can have huge repercussions on the whole climbing community - in life, all adherents to an activity are generally lumped in the same bag. Careless actions or a disregard for rules and regulations, however irksome and seemingly unnecessary they may be, could lead to a prime climbing area being closed to generations of climbers.

If in doubt, always contact the local Mountain or Alpine Club, which is usually in the best position to give you informed, up-to-date information and opinions.

Opposite left Top-roping encourages the safe development of skills.

Opposite right Climbing at any level can be exhilarating.

ALPINE CLIMBING – INCORPORATING SNOW AND ICE CLIMBING

For the first time, the elements of snow and ice enter into the equation. In this discipline, climbers face the full spectrum of mountain experiences: crevasses, avalanches, extreme cold, bad weather, loose rock, and serious time constraints. In alpine climbing, speed is often of the essence in order to take advantage of good ice or snow conditions, and breaks in the weather. Rules are less stringent, and using pieces of gear for aid is not frowned on. Success often means merely surviving. (*See* page 132.)

Far left Careful planning has always been a feature of successful expeditions, such as the 1953 Everest expedition, shown here.

Left Moving up the ridge on Ancohuma in the Andes; the climbers are sensibly well back from the edge.

EXPEDITIONS

Expeditions to major peaks such as the 8000m ones, or many lower but equally challenging peaks, are in many ways the zenith of climbing. Here the rules are simple – do it, any which way, and come back. Having said this, the expedition game has slowly developed its own set of categories, including oxygenless ascents, ascents without sherpas, and the super-alpine game which involves applying fast alpine-style pushes to the great peaks, such as the South Face route on Aconcagua in the Argentine Andes (which is regarded as the biggest face in the Americas), or even rapid solos of Everest. Each of these raises the stakes, and makes the challenge ever more difficult, the outcome ever less certain.

Whatever the level you are at or aiming for, you will never regret having become a mountaineer.

CATHERINE DESTIVELLE

Catherine Destivelle has succeeded in making her mark as one of the world's top alpinists and climbers in what has traditionally been regarded as a 'man's world'.

Catherine was born in 1960 in French Algeria. As a young child she was captivated watching the bouldering at Fontainebleau in France, and pestered her father until she was allowed to join him climbing. At 16 she was already recognized as a climbing prodigy, leading routes in Chamonix, including the American Direct Route on the Petit Dru. Catherine then turned to sport and competition climbing, winning the prestigious Bardoneccia event for two consecutive years, and the World Championship title for four. She abandoned competition climbing shortly after this and returned to natural rock.

Her accomplishments include climbing the isolated and demanding Nameless Tower in the Karakorum, with Jeff Lowe; a solo ascent of the North Face of the Eiger in winter in a near-record 15 hours; the Bonatti Pillar on the Dru, solo in four hours; and the Bonatti route on the North Face of the Matterhorn, solo – as well as countless other hard routes on rock and in alpine areas.

Right *Catherine Destivelle leads a pitch at Point Perpendicular, New South Wales, Australia.*

WOMEN AND CLIMBING

In the history of world mountaineering, women have perhaps not featured as heavily as one might expect. The reasons are numerous, not the least being the 'macho' image with which climbing and related activities have been associated. In many sports, women were traditionally held to be 'incapable' of exceptional achievements, and mountaineering was (and perhaps to some extent, unfortunately, still is) no exception.

There are argued to be genuine physical reasons why women mountaineers and climbers do not have as rich a history as men. However, the modern exploits of figures such as France's Catherine Destivelle, solo on the Dru; Britain's Alison Hargreaves' peak-bagging record in the Himalayas before her untimely death; the Chinese women's expedition to Everest; and the American women's expedition to Annapurna in the Himalayas, all prove that women can be as capable as men in the mountaineering world.

Between 1911 and 1944, the Frenchwoman Alexandra David-Neel journeyed to high areas, including many high-altitude peaks and passes in Tibet, all alone and disguised as a beggar-woman. The Americans Fanny Bullock and Annie Peck made high-altitude ascents in the early 1900s, with the 58-year-old Annie ascending the 6656m (21,838ft) Andean peak of Huascaran – an 'all American record' – in 1908.

In 1934, Hettie Dyhrenfurth, a Swiss-American, climbed the aptly named Queen Mary Peak (7428m; 24,371ft) in the Karakorum, northern Kashmir, to claim the new female altitude record. Women first went over 8000m in 1974, when three members of the

Japanese women's expedition climbed the Nepalese peak of Manaslu (8153m; 26,750ft). In 1975 Wanda Rutkiewicz and Alison Chadwick-Onyskiewicz led a mixed Polish expedition up Gasherbrum III in the Himalayas, then the highest unclimbed peak in the world. At the same time, Anna Okopinska and Halina Syrokomska ascended Gasherbrum II – the first time that women, unaccompanied by men, had summitted over 8000 metres.

In recent years, women have increasingly made their mark in all spheres of climbing, from competitions to expeditions.

Above Lynn Hill, in action at the Berkeley World Cup, has often set the women's standards for extreme rock routes.

Left Robyn Erbesfield displays the style that made her world champion for four consecutive years.

CHAPTER TWO

THE CLIMBER'S ENVIRONMENT

Ours to Care For

'One man's mountain is another man's mole-hill': this is truer today than ever before, as climbers explore the possibilities inherent in a vast range of environments. To the confirmed city dweller a small local crag can be their 'Everest', and summitting it a risky undertaking; to an experienced Himalayan climber, the local hills which challenge so many may not even be worth a second glance.

While mountaineering is often associated with risk, particularly in the eyes of the insurance world, most mountain experiences (local or alpine) contain less risk than crossing the local high street. Regardless of their size, however, mountains share certain common characteristics – chief among these being the sensitivity of their deceptively robust ecosystems to the impact of human intervention.

It is, perhaps, the seemingly eternal montane environments which are more at risk from climbers than vice versa. Climbers should treat their climbing environment with the same care with which they prepare and equip themselves to climb if they wish to preserve the beauty and integrity of such areas, and keep them accessible for climbing.

Llamas are used to transport equipment in parts of South America.

WILDLIFE

Mountains are home to unique species that find refuge in the inaccessibility of their faces, be they tiny frogs, such as Cape Town's Table Mountain ghost frog which lives on the slopes of this city mountain, or the elusive snow leopard of the Himalayas (not to mention the Yeti!).

Enjoying the solitude in the Arthur Range, in southwest Tasmania.

The rare Lampranthus maximiliani *is found high on sandstone rock sheets.*

Mountains are rightly considered to be rugged places and the plants and animals that inhabit them are often correspondingly rugged, as they have to deal with extreme temperatures, high winds, and often low oxygen levels.

Unique species exist that have, for example, adapted to very high levels of ultraviolet light, that have developed white camouflage for snow conditions, or that can get by with minimal oxygen. Certain of the Andean vultures have specialized haemoglobin which has a tremendously high oxygen-carrying capacity, while the sure-footedness of the chamois (a species of mountain antelope) is a joy to behold.

The ruggedness of the mountains is misleading, as their ecology can be extremely fragile. The layer of soil is often thin, tenuously adhering to a hard substrate at near-critical angles. There are few level areas for the development of lush growths, and the changing of seasons brings about harsh conditions for survival. Plant and animal populations are often small, and a minute change in habitat can have devastating consequences.

With the current pressures of overpopulation and pollution on the mountainous areas of the world, this fragile ecology is being threatened and species are dying out at a frightening rate.

It is important that climbers realize this and adopt procedures to avoid damaging the environment. Much has been made of the litter left behind by many expeditions to the giant peaks, and this is certainly of consequence. It is, however, perhaps less important than a number of other considerations which are often glossed over:

SOME NEGATIVE IMPACTS
• The numbers of tourists and climbers impact on the mountain vegetation; whole forests are being stripped to make fires or to act as load-carrying poles in Kenya and the Karakorum.
• Constant human traffic cuts down on the hunting time available to predators, leading to upsurges in their prey populations which then destroy vegetation and denude hillsides. This is evident in some areas of North Africa and Asia.
• Whole areas of natural vegetation are cut down to make way for crops to feed the 'visitors', and herd animals are brought in, replacing the natural antelope which have served as a sustainable food source for generations.
• The money and porterage 'work' brought in by climbers, along with improved medical care, has led to escalating human population pressures in many mountain ranges, further taxing the resources of their fragile ecologies.

Nowhere is safe from human pollution, as is evident from the amounts of litter found around many base camps.

• The degradation of the soil at the base of some pressurized small climbing crags – such as Stanage in Britain, Ceuse in France, Arco in Italy, and Boulder in the USA, to name but a few – cannot simply be ignored. Paths are deeply eroded and entire areas have been denuded of vegetation. Arguments claiming that only a few areas are affected and that most of the environment is left untouched may be true, but the number of climbers is rising rapidly, and more and more areas will suffer the same fate if the problem is left unchecked. The recent closure of whole areas to climbers in Germany should be a salutary lesson – take care of the environment, or you will lose access.

• Many climbers tend to be rather cavalier in their treatment of mountains, especially high mountains, feeling that there is nothing up there to disturb. Yet on some of the highest rocks in the world, tiny colonies of lichens, that unique symbiotic association of algae and fungi, have been discovered.

An awareness of these problems and positive steps taken to minimize their effects will help to preserve the mountains and their delicate living creatures as we know them for future generations, while ensuring that climbers retain access to their areas of activity.

ENVIRONMENT-FRIENDLY CLIMBING

• Flora and fauna should be left undisturbed, from the tiny fragile plant in a crack on your local crag to the mountain goats of the Himalayas.

• More 'closed' plant and animal sanctuaries need to be established, which allow only minimal human intervention. The sanctity of mountain sanctuaries should be respected.

• Climbing bans in areas of ecological significance, or temporary bans for bird nesting and other environmental reasons, must be upheld.

• Climbers should carry in their own food and carry out their waste.

• Increased self-sufficiency for climbers will also reduce the pressure currently generated by the many hundreds of porters in the major ranges.

• Climbers could support education campaigns to promote a realistic approach to sensible human population control.

• A full management policy for crags should be insisted on by climbers, who should be pro-active and not merely uncaring or at best 'supportive'. In this way, climbers will retain access to the areas they so dearly love.

• Climbers must respect the wishes of landowners.

• Climbers should consider local feelings and ethics with respect to bolting, 'chipping' and 'cleaning' of rock faces (*see* panel).

ALTERATION OF THE NATURAL ROCK

A very controversial issue at present is the 'improvement' of natural rock to either enhance the quality of climbs or make it possible to climb short sections of a route that would otherwise be unclimbable. To some extent, climbers have always 'improved' the rock – by removing loose flakes or stones to make passage safer, by using pitons or other points of aid, or by drilling bolts.

A current trend, largely associated with the cutting edge of sport climbing (where harder and harder routes are sought on limited expanses of suitable rock), is that of either 'chipping' holds in blank sections of rock or glueing on small pieces of stone (or even man-made climbing grips) to make the route feasible. Sometimes the former is excused as 'cleaning' the rock while the latter is referred to as 'replacing broken sections'!

This will doubtless remain a heated issue for a good number of years to come.

Top A crowded crag in the Chamonix valley which has been denuded of foliage.

Left Many Bolivian people still follow traditional ways, despite the influx of climbers and tourists.

LOCAL POPULATIONS

The question of the effect climbers have on local indigenous populations is an interesting one. In developed areas, climbing generates an income for guides, hostels, trade and industry. Apart from the resultant seasonal crowding and perhaps a certain loss of charm, few would argue that the boom in climbing has done serious harm to the residents of places such as Chamonix, France.

However, in the mountains of less developed countries, the questions become more searching. Local populations are exposed to 'wealthy' Western climbers, and all the trappings of civilization. These are generally so far out of the locals' reach that both greed and resentment develop, and often the very fabric of their society alters.

Hand-in-hand with the visitors come Western education, religion, entertainment and health care. The resultant changes in population dynamics, over-population, loss of tradition and family break-up are easily overlooked.

Climbers and trekking companies, together with the governments of the countries concerned need to examine this issue closely and objectively in order to lessen the adverse effects of too-rapid change. Certainly no-one would want to hold back the advancement of a culture or group of people. This having been said, however, the current system of hand-outs and non-sustainable flushes of wealth are no basis for sound development. Similarly, a health-care system which enables more children to survive into adulthood in a society which offers them no prospect of future employment or land, and where families cannot afford to feed the 'extra' mouths, is not always the blessing it sets out to be.

Far left Llamas can be temperamental, and delicate equipment should be packed carefully to survive their tricks.

Left Bolivian children watch a climber preparing his meal. Their curiosity about Western-style food and goods often disrupts their well-established, traditional way of life.

MOUNTAIN WEATHER

Mountain ranges are notorious for their rapid weather changes. The sides of mountains deflect winds, causing clouds and rain in their vicinity. During the day, as the air warms, it expands and rises up the slopes, referred to as a 'valley breeze'. As this air rises, it cools by 1°C (2°F) every 100m (330ft). The fast-rising air cools adiabatically (the term given to cooling by expansion resulting from a drop in pressure). This drop in temperature often leads to cloud formation as the pressure of the water vapour alters, leading to condensation.

Late in the day, the air cools further and moves downwards – the 'mountain breeze' – dispersing the clouds, often leading to the summer rainstorms characteristic of many mountainous regions.

Short-term instabilities can cause sudden and unexpected rainstorms, and meteorologists are understandably wary of predicting mountain weather on a local, short-term basis. Peaks such as the Eiger in Switzerland, standing at the edge of a range, have their own weather patterns which vary with lightning rapidity. Various areas are also affected by long-term air movements, with high- and low-

pressure systems tending to 'migrate' north or south in different seasons. For instance, the Azores anti-cyclone which dominates the weather in central Europe in summer produces a semi-permanent high-pressure system. This generates weather cycles of 10 to 12 fine days, followed by a few days of stormy weather, as a result of interaction with the low-pressure system predominating over western Europe and Asia. Generally, the weather stabilizes for a month or so in September to October. Similar 'cycles' can be identified in most mountain areas, and climbers are well advised to take cognizance of these when planning their trip.

An altimeter-barometer is a useful short-term predictor. Once at a fixed altitude, any rise or fall over a number of hours can indicate weather trends. A significant fall in pressure (shown as a 'rise' in altitude) predicts bad weather; the faster the drop, the more violent the storm is likely to be. Conversely a steady rise in pressure (a 'drop' in altitude) will herald an improvement in the weather.

The high peaks of the world project into the jet stream, the name given to the fast-moving wind belts at the edge of the breathable atmosphere. This can

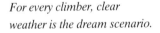
For every climber, clear weather is the dream scenario.

lead to winds with speeds in excess of 160kph (100mph) with drastic consequences for climbers. Choosing the 'right' time of the year in terms of wind and weather patterns can dictate success or failure in the mountains. This is particularly true of the big ranges such as the Andes or Himalayas.

LIGHTNING

Mountains frequently give rise to lightning storms – spectacular if you are far away, terrifying if you are uncomfortably close. Peaks and ridges produce the vertical updrafts and raincloud conditions that generate lightning, and climbers thus often find themselves in the strike zone.

Electrical potential builds up in clouds in much the same way that we generate it by rubbing nylon against nylon on a dry day. Electrons are transferred from one molecule to another as the air masses rush past one another or past the earth. Air is normally a poor conductor, whereas earth, trees, rock and the human body are better conductors. Because air offers little by way of a pathway, an imbalance of electrons builds up, creating a 'potential difference' or 'charge'. Any electrical charge follows physical laws which tend to neutralize it, or 'balance the charge'.

The accumulated electrons which constitute the charge will find the course of least resistance in order to achieve electrical balance. Because of the mutual repulsion of differing charges, the electrons tend to stream towards a 'point density' on the outside of a charged surface – for example a rock tower, a tree or a human head (*see* illustration).

A phenomenon sometimes seen is 'St Elmo's Fire' – a bluish-tinged corona accompanied by humming or crackling sounds. Often metal equipment starts to 'sing' or your hair stands on end. Although this does not indicate a definite strike where you is standing, it should be sufficient warning to encourage evasive action! Even a strike a few metres away will generate sufficient free electrons to move a good few billion through your body. This shock can disrupt the action of the heart, knock out brain activity, or cause severe burns. When lightning threatens, climbers should:
• Avoid moist areas, such as gullies and cracks.
• Sit or crouch on insulated objects, such as a kit bag or rope.
• Avoid ridges, stay off the top.

• Keep out of overhangs or small caves – lightning may strike the ground via you from the cave roof.
• On a ledge, crouch at the outer edge. Tie on via a short lead.
• Try to find an area with something a bit above your head height, e.g. a small tree or rock.
• Move away from metal objects if possible – they do not 'attract' a strike, but might intensify the effect via induced currents.
If someone is struck by lightning you should begin cardiopulmonary resuscitation, and treat the burns.

Above Looking down from the heights on the storm below.

Overleaf A climber reads the summit records on Namibia's Spitskop. Keeping summit records is a fascinating tradition.

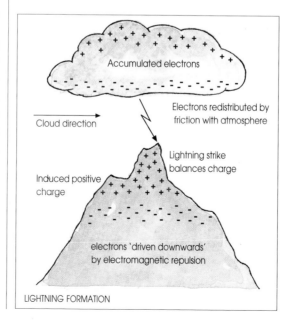

LIGHTNING FORMATION

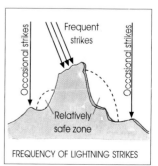

FREQUENCY OF LIGHTNING STRIKES

Granite

Limestone

Dolomite

Slate

Sandstone

THE STRUCTURE OF MOUNTAINS

There are several types of rock, all of which pose various challenges to the climber.

ROCK TYPES AND TYPICAL ASSOCIATED CLIMBING

Granite: as a result of the differences in formation produced during the volcanic upwelling of lava that creates this granular, crystalline rock, a wide range of rock consistencies occur; from the compact, solid granites of Half-Dome in Yosemite, via coarser-grained Alpine rock, to the loose horrors found in countries such as Greece and Malawi.

Granite climbs tend to require either frictioning on slabs (*see* page 77), with the granite crystals affording purchase (or causing a cheesegrater effect if the climber comes off!); or making use of crack lines, which demands good finger-, foot-, hand- or even body-jamming techniques (*see* pages 51, 52).

Limestone: formed from the calcareous skeletons of underwater creatures, it is easily eroded by water and by reaction with the carbon dioxide in the air. This produces small 'finger-cup' pockets for climbers to use, as in Verdon, France, or on the dripstone formations found in Thailand. Placing protection (*see* page 78) on limestone can be tricky as it is soft and often friable, and drilled-in bolts are popular.

MAJOR MOUNTAIN FEATURES
Incorporating some typical routes. Squares indicate base camps or huts and circles show advance camps or bivouacs.

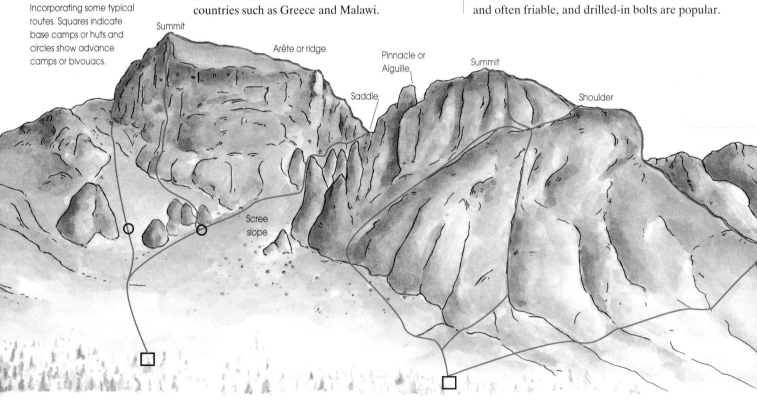

Summit

Arête or ridge

Pinnacle or
Aiguille

Saddle

Summit

Shoulder

Scree
slope

Quartzite

Dolerite

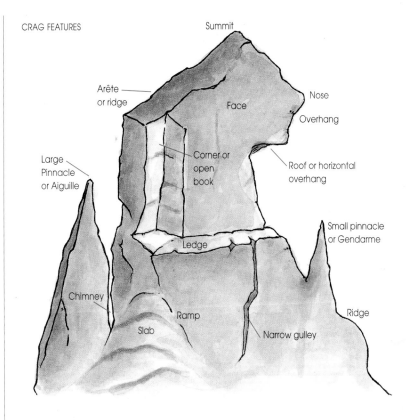

CRAG FEATURES

Summit

Arête or ridge

Face

Nose

Overhang

Corner or open book

Roof or horizontal overhang

Large Pinnacle or Aiguille

Ledge

Small pinnacle or Gendarme

Chimney

Ramp

Ridge

Slab

Narrow gulley

Dolomite: less compact than limestone, dolomite comes in layers or 'chunks' which enables natural protection to be used more easily. The spectacular towers and faces of the European Alps and the Italian and Austrian Dolomites are typical of dolomite rock formation.

Slate: a smooth and difficult rock to master, slate climbing can be nerve-racking, providing little to stand on or hold onto, and dubious protection placement. Even bolts are unreliable as slate, by its very nature, peels off in large blocks – taking protection and climber with it! The slate quarries of Wales are the true testing ground for the slate enthusiast.

Sandstone: this is probably, with granite, the most abundant rock type. Sandstone comes in a wide variety of textures and forms. It can be soft and fine-grained, as in the southern English and German sandstones; melted together into the coarse-grained gritstones found in the Peak District of England; or compact sandstone as in America's desert spires, the

Ridge

Cape sandstones of southern Africa, and those of Australia's Blue Mountains. In general, sandstone provides moderately good friction and it often has distinct crack lines – and thus affords solid protection placements.

Quartzite: a more solid form of fused sandstone, which has been metamorphosed by volcanic action. This produces good 'rails' (horizontal cracks) and vertical cracks, and also allows for the placement of natural gear (*see* page 82). Quartzite is found in many parts of the world; some of the most popular sites are in Spain and the east coast of North America. Australia's Arapiles (Djurid), one of the world's most famous cliffs, is made up of a dense, solid quartzite.

Dolerite, basalt, schist, gneiss: these metamorphosed rocks often have loose aggregates and a coarse texture, and are therefore not always popular rock types for climbers. Nonetheless, these rocks comprise quite a large part of the base of a number of major mountain ranges, such as the Himalayas and ranges in South America, and they can provide good – although nerve-racking – climbing.

THE STRUCTURE OF GLACIERS

The long-term accumulation of unmelted snow gives rise to glaciers. If the angle of the slope is right, then it compacts into ice, and slowly starts to move downhill. By a process called 'firnification' the air-filled snow-ice, or névé, is turned to true glacier ice, which is so compact that very little air is trapped. Under the action of constant melting and refreezing during the seasons, and because of pressure effects on the ice, the glacier ice starts to have different consistencies.

Right Great care must be taken when approaching a crevasse as many broaden out under a narrow entrance. This climber should be roped up.

Below Glaciers are slow but powerful shapers of rock.

While many tons of ice accumulate on a glacier each year, it also melts away at the glacier's snout. The temperature of the lower valley causes melting, and ice ablates (evaporates) from the surface of the glacier. A glacier has thixotropic properties – that is, it is a solid behaving in some ways like a liquid. The centre, for instance, 'flows' faster than the edges, as the edges experience drag from friction with the surrounding rocks. This causes the glacier to break up and leads to the formation of crevasses in moving glaciers. The surface, being under less pressure, tends to be more solid, and the stress on this as the glacier 'bends' over convexities (bulges) in the ground beneath leads to transverse crevasses.

The first transverse crevasse, occurring where the glacier tears itself away from the upper rock edge, is called the bergschrund. This is often either the first or last real problem on a climb, as it can be difficult and dangerous to cross.

Some glaciers in Greenland move at up to 20m (65ft) per day, but speeds of a few centimetres to a few metres a day are more usual. Glaciers have been responsible for much of the shaping and erosion of valleys in the history of the formation of the earth's surface. They are powerful and emotive features of mountains, the crevasses, moraines, bergschrunds, séracs, groans and grumbles all adding excitement to the life of the mountaineer.

The snout of a South American glacier affords climbers some enjoyable ice climbing.

CHAPTER THREE

ROCK CLIMBING ESSENTIALS
Tools of the Trade

Much of the basic equipment and many of the basic principles are central to all kinds of climbing, from short, easy rock climbs to long alpine faces and big walls.

It has already been indicated that climbing is not a death-wish activity, thus to climb and survive injury-free should be the aim of every responsible person.

Climbing readiness is vital and can be divided into two main spheres:

– personal readiness (both mental and physical)

– equipment readiness (quality and knowledge of proper usage).

Personal readiness implies that one has made up one's mind to do a certain type of climb. If you have decided to take on an ascent of The Nose on El Capitan, Yosemite, then you must ensure that you have all of the skills and the abilities required: a head for heights, patience, good judgement, tolerance of your partner, and incredible determination. Add to this familiarity with all of the technical equipment you will need, a wide range of practised climbing skills, and great physical fitness.

Chalk bag

Mental readiness is more complex but in the end often comes down to confidence, and that in turn comes from considerable experience.

'I try to avoid risks. I think it's possible to do so with everyday training, technical training, psychological training' (Tomo Cesen after his claimed solo ascent of Lhotse South Face, 8511m; 27,924ft).

Long routes often require a considerable amount of equipment.

Selection of ropes

Equipment readiness comes from both handling the equipment frequently, and knowing the practical and theoretical benefits and limits of each piece of your gear. Being familiar with the equipment will decrease mental stress, which in turn will enhance your general enjoyment and performance, as well as increasing your safety margins.

Be sure to practise putting equipment on, tying knots, placing and removing gear, clipping it on and off your harness or bandoliers, at home or in a safe environment before heading for that intimidating crag.

AROUSAL AND CLIMBING

The human body is complex, controlled by our conscious decisions and by background influences from the autonomic nervous and glandular systems. The latter two interact continuously and, in concert with our conscious side (and the information we are receiving from the outside world), keep us moving, alive and alert.

'Arousal' here refers to the body's psychological and physical 'state of readiness' to respond to challenges in the surroundings – the 'fight or flight' syndrome. The autonomic nervous system, in response to conscious arousal (e.g. fear, thrill, excitement) alters the balance of two hormones – adrenaline and noradrenaline – secreted by the adrenal medulla of the brain.

Adrenaline is secreted in response to psychological and physical stress, and causes the heartbeat to rise, breathing to become shallower but faster, the capillaries to open, internal muscle tension to increase, and the blood sugar level to rise.

These responses can be an asset to the climber, but negative effects include less oxygen in the muscles in the long term, loss of fine motor coordination, increased sweating (slippery hands), and a heightened perception of the here-and-now which reduces longer-term planning and forethought. Excessive arousal thus hampers technique and will squander both valuable energy and mental resources.

Climbers should learn to control their arousal levels – through familiarity with the activity (resulting in less fear), and through making use of conscious control and calming mechanisms. For instance, you should take a few minutes before climbing a pitch to breathe properly – slowly and deeply – and to visualize your opening moves calmly and confidently.

STARTING OUT

These days it is becoming increasingly acceptable for climbers to start off by doing a course. In doing this, the beginner learns a good deal, rapidly and in a structured form. Alternatively, many prefer the do-it-yourself method. It is wisest, however, to make use of some form of expertise. Associating with experienced climbers and watching their moves is a good supplement to a book like this. Most climbers are friendly folk, and will readily offer advice.

Left A long, serious route in the Verdon Gorge, France, produces maximum arousal.

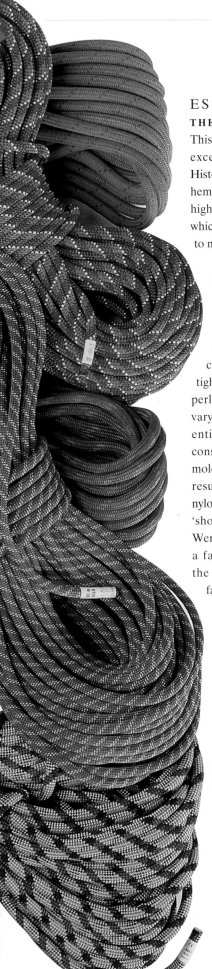

ESSENTIAL EQUIPMENT

THE ROPE

This is the common element of all 'real' climbing, except for bouldering and solo free climbs. Historically, ropes have developed from the original hemp or manila ropes, which had little strength and high weight and bulk, via hawser-laid nylon ropes, which afforded a little more protection to the leader, to modern composite ropes.

The early ropes were little more than aids to the second climber or useful in descent, as they were ineffective in braking a falling leader. The motto was thus 'the leader does not fall'.

These days, the only rope taken seriously by climbers is the kernmantel rope. In this, the core of more elastic fibres is surrounded by a tightly woven protective sheath. Bundles of nylon, perlon or similar polyamide fibres are woven into varying patterns. Each fibre is continuous for the entire length of the rope, and each visible fibre consists of thousands of intertwined single-chain molecules. Every rope has an elongation property, resulting from the molecular construction of the nylon, and the weave. It is this that gives the rope its 'shock absorption' property in the case of a fall. Were the rope not to absorb the forces generated in a fall gradually, the resulting jolt could break the back of a climber in even surprisingly short falls of a few metres.

The Rope and Energy Absorption

Few realize that the major purpose of the rope is to dissipate the energy (E) resulting from a fall or generated in an abseil. The formula:

$$E_{potential} = \text{mass x gravitational constant} \\ \text{x height}$$

gives the amount of energy to be converted during a fall or an abseil.

An 80kg person abseiling 10m has mass x gravitational constant x distance = energy units i.e. 80kg x 9.8m/s x 10m = 7840J or 7.8kJ

During a fall, this formula becomes:

$$E_{kinetic} = \tfrac{1}{2} \text{ mass x velocity}^2$$

This energy has to be released from the system (a 'system' refers to the climber[s] and all intervening links and gear placements), and is often released in the form of heat, including heat generated in the rope as fibres twist and unwind.

In the example, 7.8kJ would raise the temperature of a litre of water some 2°C, or the temperature of your abseil device by quite a few degrees, as many a singed hand will testify! (*See* also the section on fall factors on page 62.)

The rope absorbs energy by elongating, and the amount and speed of this is determined by a complex interaction between the macromolecular structure and the braiding pattern. Each rope type and manufacturer makes use of a slightly different set of criteria, and thus different ropes are more applicable to certain situations than others.

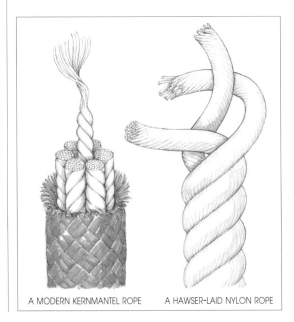

A MODERN KERNMANTEL ROPE   A HAWSER-LAID NYLON ROPE

Buying a Rope

Factors of importance in buying a rope include:

Length: ropes can be bought in any length, from centimetres to kilometres! The most usual lengths

Kernmantel rope fibres

are 50m (165ft) for double or twin rope technique and most sport climbing, although 60m (200ft) ropes are increasingly being used on sport crags such as Ceuse, Verdon and Buoux in France, as well as in other parts of the world.

Diameter: 10.5 or 11mm diameter ropes are referred to in UIAA standards as 'full ropes', indicating that they can be used on their own; 9 and 8.5mm ropes are called 'half ropes', implying that the leader needs to use two of these to have a safe system. Full ropes and half ropes are labelled '1' or '½' respectively on tapes at the end of a rope.

Smaller diameter ropes, such as 6mm or 8mm, are used for prusik slings (*see* page 92), pack hauling, and even as fixed ropes on large peaks where weight is critical.

Type: apart from minor variations in manufacturing specifications, kernmantel ropes come in two major types: dynamic and static.

Dynamic ropes are standard, energy-absorbing climbing ropes. These usually have a white core (dyeing slightly reduces fibre strength) and a dyed outer sheath for easy identification as well as to reduce the effect of ultraviolet rays, and to help show abrasion and rope damage.

Static ropes are made from a different nylon and are often braided differently to give a tighter weave. They have minimal stretch, and are useful for abseiling, caving or ascending, but they do not absorb shock, so are not safe for leading or even serious top-roping. Most static ropes are white, with coloured identification stripes.

Handling properties: a balance has to be struck between suppleness, knotability, and easy coiling. A more flexible, softer rope handles better, but because of its more loosely woven sheath, it is likely to wear sooner as a result of abrasion.

Abrasion resistance: a tightly woven sheath gives greater abrasion resistance, but adversely affects both handling and weight.

Water-shedding properties: ropes are not damaged or even weakened by water but, when wet, both their weight and handling characteristics are altered. A further danger is that ice may form from absorbed water, and the crystals may cut or damage rope fibres during use. The fibres of 'Everdry' ropes are treated with a silicone or Teflon coating during manufacture, making them much less absorbent. These are useful for wet, icy or snowy conditions.

CAUTION

Static ropes are not safe for leading or for top-roping where falls of even 0.5m (1.6ft) or more are expected. They transmit an unacceptably high force to the harness and climber in the event of a fall.

Opposite top Friction on sharp edges can cause ropes to fray.

Spectra accessory cord

Accessory cord

Accessory cord

Thicker accessory cord

Static rope

9mm rope – note the '½' marking

9.5mm rope

10mm rope

11mm rope – note the '1' marking

Far left 'Everdry' ropes are easier to handle in snow.

Bent and straightgate
opengate carabiners

CARABINERS

Carabiners are used as links in the 'climbing chain' or 'system'. A climbing chain generally consists of two climbers, linked to one another by a rope which may be tied directly to each. Usually the situation is more complex: each climber wears a harness, with the rope tied directly to this or clipped in via a carabiner.

Carabiners serve to connect various components together – the climber to a sling, the sling to a piece of equipment placed in the rock, and so on. They are easy to open and close and extremely strong, and are vital components of modern climbing. They come in a variety of shapes and sizes, but essentially three common types are recognized:

Opengate: these have no locking mechanism and are used on running belays (*see* panel above) or where the rope cannot easily flick out of the carabiner. The advantages are lighter weight and a quick action – useful in leading hard routes. The disadvantage is that the rope can flick out of these, particularly in falls, where vibrations can lead to the rope 'bouncing' out of a carabiner as its gate rapidly opens and closes under rope action. This is more common than many climbers imagine. In extreme situations, some form of locking device is important. An alternative is to double up on carabiners, with their gates reversed.

Screwgate: there are various types, all of which have a gate with a locking mechanism to ensure that the carabiner cannot accidentally open. They are often used to attach the rope to the climber or main belays. Lightness is forfeited for security.

Twistlock: new auto-locking gate actions are becoming popular, particularly in instructional situations, to prevent accidental gate unlocking. These are finding favour with climbers because of the extra security they offer with little trade-off in lightness.

RUNNING BELAYS

Running belays, or 'runners', consist of pieces of equipment placed or found in the rock into which the leader clips the rope via a carabiner as he climbs past. This system safeguards both the leader and the second climber in the event of a fall.

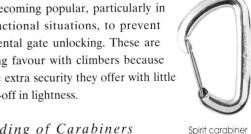

Spirit carabiner

Loading of Carabiners

Carabiners are designed to take the load along their major axis, or length. A carabiner rated at 20kN (2000kg) along the spine will often only be 6kN across the minor axis. Three-way loading dramatically increases the chances of failure in severe fall situations.

Carabiner gates can be pushed open by resting against the rock, or vibrated open by rope action during falls. You only have to watch some high-speed film footage of carabiners vibrating open and protection systems whipping around during a fall situation to appreciate the potential for disaster. Screwgates and lockgates will help you to overcome this problem.

Twistlock carabiner

Care of Carabiners

To allow full movement of the gate, carabiners should be cleaned periodically with warm water, liquid soap and a brush. Moving parts should be treated with silicone (not oil, which may damage other climbing equipment). Many lightweight alloy carabiners are susceptible to corrosion. You should be wary of a carabiner that has held a serious fall, or that has been dropped some way onto a hard surface; invisible deformation could have taken place.

Traditional
screwgate
carabiner

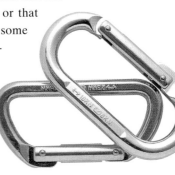

Plain and oval-D
opengate carabiners

Auto-locking carabiner

HARNESSES

The choice of harness is partly a matter of personal preference, partly of its intended function.

Lightweight harnesses find favour with sport and competition climbers, where every gram counts; padded and adjustable harnesses are favoured by those on longer routes, comfort being traded for weight on hanging belays; and adjustable leg loops are favoured for alpine or snow conditions. Full-body harnesses are the choice of many alpinists, and for very young children, who might slip out of a waist-belt-type harness.

Certain principles apply to all types of harness:

Size of waist belt: large enough to accommodate extra clothing if required, small enough to ensure a tight fit when climbing.

Size of leg loops: sufficient to enable freedom of leg movement.

Gear loops: sufficient for intended use – fewer for sport climbing, more substantial ones and in greater number for ice and snow work.

Padding: waist belts and leg loops need padding to maintain blood circulation if the wearer intends spending a good deal of time hanging in the harness, e.g. for aid climbing or hanging belays. Weight is traded for comfort. New technology has generated very light, comfortable harnesses with well-padded

Alpine-style harness

waist belts and leg loops. Extra price is balanced by long-term user-friendliness.

HELMETS

Although regarded by many climbers as 'a bit old-fashioned' and generally not felt to be required in sport or in top-rope climbing, most climbers would agree that they have a vital role in climbing on crags and longer routes, and certainly in the Alps or bigger mountains where stonefall or icefall is likely. Many a good climber has come to an untimely end as a result of not wearing a helmet. Modern helmets are becoming lighter and more comfortable, without having sacrificed strength.

Child's full-body harness

LIFESPAN OF CLIMBING EQUIPMENT

All climbing equipment is subject to deterioration with age, even if hanging totally unused in a dark, dry cupboard. Corrosion insidiously works on metal, while nylon and plastic lose elasticity and strength. Any piece of climbing gear has a limited life span so beware of using your friend's rope which has hung unused in a room for 15 years!

Metal objects older than 10 years must be treated with caution as a result of possible corrosion effects (carabiners, figure 8 descendeurs, nuts, and other aluminium composites are particularly susceptible). Nylon, perlon, plastic and similar materials (used in ropes, slings, harnesses, helmets, etc.) older than five years will be diminished in resilience and strength. Your old rope and harness might be fine for top-roping on the local crag, but beware of leading a serious route with the same equipment.

The more an object has been used, the faster the probable deterioration. Ropes, tapes and slings can lose their elasticity – and thus their vital shock-absorption property – at a frightening rate, even when unused.

Lightweight, ventilated carbon-fibre helmet

Modern glass-fibre helmet

CAUTION

Always fully double back the straps in the buckles when putting the harness on. Many climbers have been injured as a result of being distracted halfway through putting on a harness, and forgetting about the essential doubling back of the waist and leg loops.

Right Old abseil slings can be dangerous – back them up with a new one.

ALPINE COIL

(a)

(b)

(c)

(d)

(e)

(f)

Used for carrying long ropes.

CLEANING AND MAINTENANCE OF EQUIPMENT

Most metal equipment can be washed in water or even a mild solvent (preferably not petroleum-based). It should be washed with soapy water, then thoroughly rinsed and dried; the use of high-pressure air to remove moisture is recommended. Moving parts can be lubricated with a silicone or Teflon lubricant, and the excess dried off.

Ropes, harnesses and the like can be washed in lukewarm water with a mild detergent – preferably a 'natural' one within a pH range of 5.5 to 8.0 – thoroughly rinsed, then allowed to dry in a cool area out of direct sunlight. Washing ropes is more for practical reasons than cosmetic ones, as it removes small pieces of grit which can damage fibres. It does, of course, also result in better-looking equipment.

All climbing gear is best stored in a cool, dry, dark cupboard. Excessive heat over a long period can speed up the ageing process.

Although some modern fibres and metals are resistant to acids and alkalis, it is absolutely essential to avoid contact with these. Beware of battery acid, petroleum, oil and similar chemicals. If in doubt, discard the equipment – a life may be at stake! Ultraviolet radiation and heat are killers of climbing gear, gradually wearing away at the nylon and plastic components.

Avoid leaving climbing gear in the sun whenever possible. Beware of trusting any sling or nylon component that has been exposed to the sun for periods of time in excess of a few days, e.g. *in situ* slings and taped nuts on crags.

Sea air is also particularly corrosive – and all equipment, particularly if metal, should be washed after prolonged exposure to salt. Encrusted salt can also damage slings and ropes.

Ropes are expensive, and need special care. A rope bag is invaluable, both to store the rope out of harm's way and to prevent kinking; the rope is simply stacked in it, not coiled. It also provides a useful platform for putting on boots, and prevents the rope from collecting sand (minute, sharp grains of sand get into the rope and can cut rope fibres slowly but surely). For this reason, avoid standing on ropes as embedded particles can cut fibres under pressure.

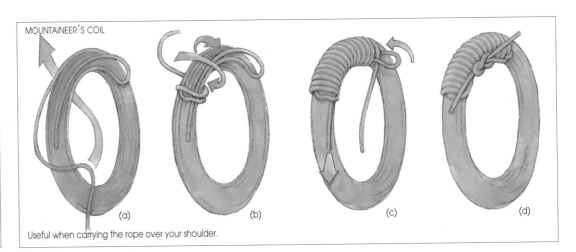

MOUNTAINEER'S COIL

(a)

(b)

(c)

(d)

Useful when carrying the rope over your shoulder.

GENERAL CLIMBING SKILLS AND TECHNIQUES

Beginners are often amazed at the ease with which experienced climbers overcome difficulties. 'Practice makes perfect' certainly applies, but personal fitness and strength also play a large role. Much of the ease of movement of old-hand climbers comes from practised techniques, with a surprising amount also stemming from familiarity with the 'engrams' (patterns of learned movement) needed to achieve certain moves.

A TWO-FINGER LOCK

A FINGER LOCK
using an opposed thumb
to stabilize the grip.

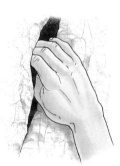

A FINGER LOCK
– often strongest with
the little finger on top.

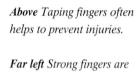

Above *Taping fingers often helps to prevent injuries.*

Far left *Strong fingers are needed for crimping.*

A PINCH GRIP

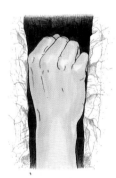

A FIST JAM

A HAND JAM

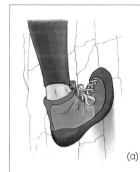

(a)

(b)

(c)

(d)

FOOT POSITIONS

(a) A foot smear uses the flat of the sole.

(b) Edging using the toe.

(c) Edging using the inner rand of the boot.

(d) Edging using the outer rand of the boot.

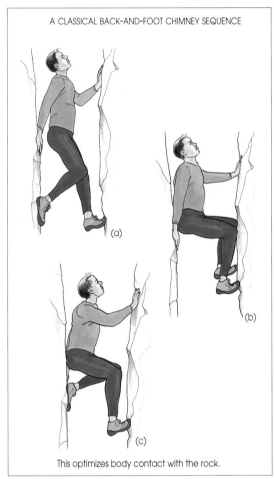

A CLASSICAL BACK-AND-FOOT CHIMNEY SEQUENCE

(a)

(b)

(c)

This optimizes body contact with the rock.

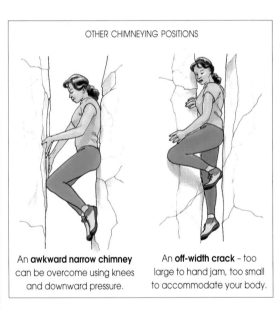

OTHER CHIMNEYING POSITIONS

An **awkward narrow chimney** can be overcome using knees and downward pressure.

An **off-width crack** – too large to hand jam, too small to accommodate your body.

Left *A climber makes light work of a chimney.*

BALANCE AND THE ART OF THE VERTICAL

Many experienced climbers save energy and strength by working 'on balance'. Standing up straight puts the weight and thus the pressure directly on your feet. Leaning into the rock diminishes the grip of your feet, putting you 'off balance'. Even under overhangs, a correct body position will reduce your energy use.

Gripping holds too tightly (a common beginner's problem) can drain energy, leading to premature 'arm-pump'. Plenty of practice lower down helps to relax one on higher, harder climbs. Bouldering and climbing walls allow for safe practice.

Certain features call for specific techniques:
Cracks: use techniques such as finger locks, hand and fist jams, foot locks or twists, or arm and elbow torqueing for larger cracks. Cracks amply illustrate the truth of the 'no pain, no gain' philosophy.
Slabs: these often call for subtlety rather than strength, although long slabs can become calf-burning torture routes. Balance is a prerequisite, making slabs popular with female climbers. Standing upright 'on balance' is usually the best approach. Often a 'long neck' helps as well, for as your protection disappears far beneath you, the 'easy angled slab' appears to defy gravity and tilt as you climb it!
Chimneying: an art that is becoming lost in the sport-climbing era, but one that is essential on the walls of Yosemite or in the European Alps. Various methods work best in different-sized chimneys, from 'thrutching' to elegant back-and-foot chimneying technique (*see* illustrations left bottom, and left top, respectively).
Overhangs: a lot of energy can be saved by efficient use of body twists, forcing the body to 'lock off' in opposition on suitable holds. Heel hooks or foot jams, once in position, can take the weight off the arms, making subsequent moves easier.

Experienced climbers save energy by using a wide range of techniques in sequence or in combination, making maximum use of every 'rest' opportunity before beginning a committing series of moves.

Right Cracks are useful places to foot jam.

TOP-ROPE ANCHORS

The basic requirement for top-roping is that access to the top of the climb is both safe and easy. The top-rope is set up by one climber climbing to the top, usually via an easy path. Experienced climbers can lead up the pitch and then anchor the rope at the top. It is then usual to abseil or walk down, unless belaying (safeguarding the other climber using the rope) from the top. Anchor points on the top can be natural (solid rock spikes or flakes or large, stable boulders around which one can pass a long sling or a spare rope), traditional gear (an experienced climber can place suitable nuts, pitons or similar) or bolted, where two or more preplaced expansion bolts afford a safe anchor point.

The belayer can either tie on at the top of the climb, then belay from the top, or the rope can be dropped down doubled, with the belayer able to belay from the bottom, next to the climber. The latter has distinct advantages, particularly when dealing with beginners, as knots and so on can be checked and advice given.

Whichever option is chosen, remember that:
• at least two points should be used to anchor the rope or belayer
• the carabiner through which the rope passes should be at least one screwgate (preferably two), or two clipgates (*see* page 58) with the gates reversed so the rope doesn't jump out by accident
• the rope should preferably start below any ledges and should not run over an edge, so that it can run freely without abrasion.

Top-roping above False Bay, South Africa. This is a good, safe way of developing your technique.

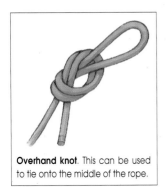

Overhand knot. This can be used to tie onto the middle of the rope.

Tying On – Knots and Attachment to Anchors
The most widely accepted knot for tying onto one's harness at the end of the rope is the figure 8, with the bowline still being used on occasion. Always ensure that the knot is tight, but not desperately so – an important part of the shock absorption of any fall is achieved by the tightening of knots.

A 'stopper knot' helps prevent the rope from accidentally working loose (which is far more common than many people realize, particularly with a larger-diameter rope).

Knots used for tying on to the middle of the rope are the figure 8 on the bight (a loop in the rope) or the overhand knot. For tying into intermediate anchors, any of the above or the clove hitch can be used. The clove hitch works well if one needs to adjust length slightly, or tie onto multiple anchors.

When belaying from above or leader belaying, it is wise to have at least two solid anchors. You should be able to share any unexpected load equally between all anchor points; lengths of rope, slings and runners should be adjusted to optimize this.

Figure 8. It is usual to tie this through all the harness safety points, and not only the front loop. Note the stopper knot in (d).

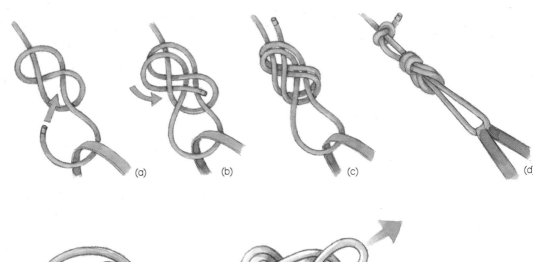

(a) (b) (c) (d)

Figure 8 on the bight. This is usually tied in the middle of the rope, or used to 'clip on' to an end.

(a) (b) (c)

Clove hitch. This enables you to adjust rope length, for instance where tying tightly onto an anchor point.

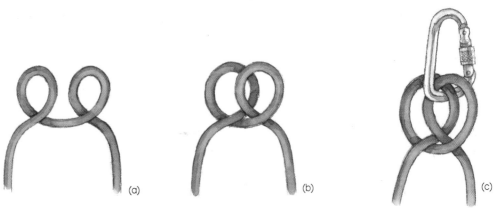

(a) (b) (c)

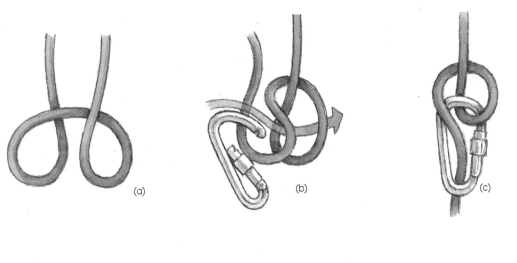

Friction (Italian) hitch. Note the braking (lower) end runs along the spine of the carabiner (diagram c), not along the gate.

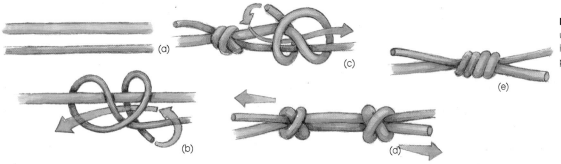

Double Fisherman's Bend. This is used to join two ropes, for instance in long double rope abseils or in a prusik loop.

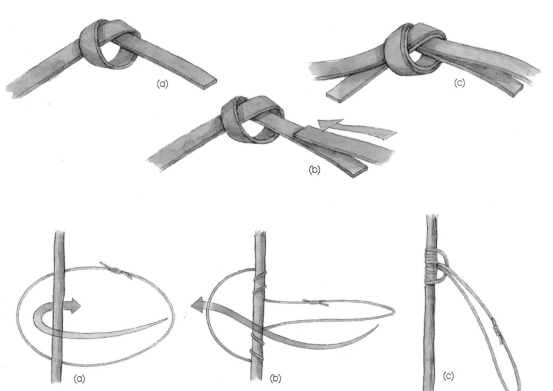

Tape knot – the only really safe way to tie a sling.

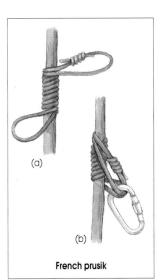

French prusik

Prusik knot. Note: the joining knot must be kept away from the rope to prevent slippage.

CAUTION

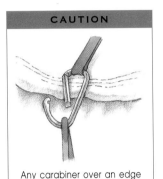

Any carabiner over an edge
is prone to gate-opening and
subsequent failure. Avoid this
by using suitable slings.

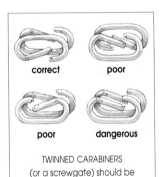

correct   poor

poor   dangerous

TWINNED CARABINERS
(or a screwgate) should be
used in top-rope situations.

*Right (from top to bottom)
Belay devices: Anka, Bug,
Betterbrake, Variable
controller, Cardiac arrester.*

*Below A Single rope controller
is useful in instructional
situations as it locks off
automatically.*

TOP-ROPING AND STARTING OUT

A good way to start climbing and to develop techniques in relative safety is via top-roping (*see* also page 22). Minimal protection-placing skills are normally required, as many areas regularly used by climbers have top-rope anchors *in situ*, or suitable trees or boulders in place. However, it is **vital** to ensure that one's top anchor system is sound, as quite considerable forces can be generated by a falling climber.

Make sure that the carabiner through which the rope finally passes is a screwgate, or even a doubled screwgate with one reversed if the carabiner is likely to touch rock, as ordinary screwgates often spin loose under repeated rope movements. Steel screwgates are worth the extra money, as their weight helps to hold the rope in place, as well as resisting wear and tear from contact with rock or rope. Ensure that the rope is free of edges and that it is running easily.

Many highly respected climbers do a lot of top-roping, so it is not a 'soft option'. Various skills are still needed – rope management, belaying, and climbing techniques. Ensure that you acquire these – either by attending a suitable course or by starting in the company of experienced climbers, who will give you guidance.

BELAYING

The safety of the roped climber depends on competent belaying. Historically, belaying began with the leader getting to the top of the climb, and then simply taking the rope in, hand over hand, for the following climbers. A rope over the shoulder was later found to be more effective, and then waist belays or belays around rock spikes came into practice.

Modern belaying uses some form of sliding knot or belaying device on a carabiner to increase the friction at the point of belay, thus stopping or reducing the fall.

Direct belays (*see* opposite) are given by putting the rope friction and force directly onto the anchor. This is done by placing the running rope around a spike or through a carabiner attached, via a sling, directly to the anchor point. In a direct belay, the belayer is 'outside the system' and does not get pulled around by the falling climber, making it suitable for climbers belaying heavier partners.

One advantage is that the belayer can easily escape from the system to effect a rescue or help the other climber. A disadvantage is that the forces generated by a falling climber impact directly onto the anchor points, which need to be correspondingly solid.

Indirect belays (*see* opposite) are more usual. Here the belaying climber ties on to the anchors, and places the rope through a belay device attached to his harness. Any forces generated by falling climbers are transmitted via the belayer to the anchor, which allows a lot of the shock to be dissipated before coming onto the anchor points. The disadvantage is that the belayer often gets pulled around, and it is more difficult for him to escape from the system if needed.

Belay Methods

Body belaying (*see* page 122) is uncommon these days but useful if working in cold conditions where the use of gloves precludes feeding the iced-up rope into belay devices, or if speed is needed and the climber is unlikely to take a serious fall. The rope passes around the back of the climber, above any attachment to an anchor if belaying from above (and vice versa). Often a carabiner clipped on to the anchor or preferably the front of the harness prevents the belay rope from being whipped too far up (or down) in a fall.

As in all belaying, the **live rope** (the rope which will brake the fall) should never be left unattended. The belayer must always keep a hand on it. Ensure that the braking hand is free to move far enough back, up or down to brake effectively. Positioning the belay so that this is assured is often neglected, despite being crucial.

Friction hitch: the simplest and yet one of the most effective devices for belaying (*see* panel, page 62) is the friction hitch (also known as the Italian hitch or Munter knot, depending on allegiances). This ideally requires a pear-shaped locking carabiner. It gives a braking force of up to 5kN (500kgf) with a normal hand pressure of about 2kN (200kgf), and is extensively used by Alpine guides and many European climbers. It can be used with one rope or, with some awkwardness, with two ropes, but a two-rope belay increases the chances of melting of the sheath (or worse) if, when holding a large fall, the two ropes are running at differential speeds. This could easily happen if, while using two ropes, the leader makes a long sideways traverse and only clips one rope into protections along his path in order to avoid rope drag. The other rope, following a more direct line up to the leader, would thus run at a different speed to that of the extended rope

Figure 8 descendeur

should the leader fall. If both ropes were under some tension and running adjacent to one another (e.g. in a friction hitch or a figure 8 belay device), then the rope-on-rope friction could melt the sheath or even the rope core.

Figure 8 descendeur: although primarily designed as an abseil device, this can be used for belaying (preferably with a single rope). However, it is often used in a number of highly suspect configurations, such as 'sport belaying' – during a fall the load can easily be turned onto the gate of the carabiner, leading to failure (*see* diagram above right).

Belay plates: these usually have two holes, designed for single or double rope belaying. The same belaying principles outlined above apply, but more practice is needed to feed two ropes through with ease.

Devices without springs, such as the Betterbrake, tend to 'jam' when feeding ropes through rapidly. A useful hint is to clip a small carabiner between the rope(s) and the belay carabiner to facilitate rope movement. This does however slightly lower the braking coefficient (*see* right, middle panel).

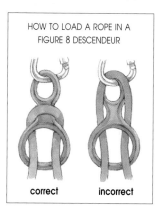

HOW TO LOAD A ROPE IN A FIGURE 8 DESCENDEUR

correct   incorrect

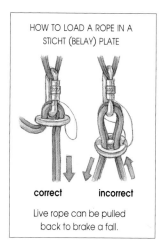

HOW TO LOAD A ROPE IN A STICHT (BELAY) PLATE

correct   incorrect

Live rope can be pulled back to brake a fall.

BELAY BODY POSITIONING

A **direct belay** avoids loading the belayer but needs a solid anchor.

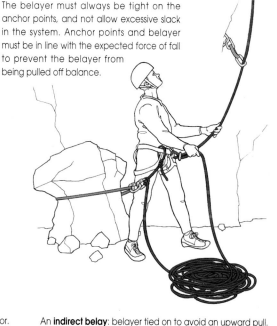

The belayer must always be tight on the anchor points, and not allow excessive slack in the system. Anchor points and belayer must be in line with the expected force of fall to prevent the belayer from being pulled off balance.

An **indirect belay**: belayer tied on to avoid an upward pull.

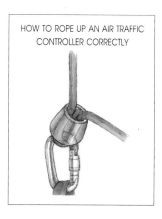

HOW TO ROPE UP AN AIR TRAFFIC CONTROLLER CORRECTLY

Above A challenging layback crack with a distinct shortage of good runners.

Right An example of good rope management on the Zing Needle, in the USA.

Below Numerous runners protect this climber.

DEVICE	SINGLE/DOUBLE ROPE	BRAKING EFFECT	GENERAL
Figure 8 descendeur	Single: any diameter	Low – beware! < 3kN (300kgf)	Still popular with many
Spring loaded Sticht plate	Single or double: usually 2 x 9mm or similar	Moderate: can feed ropes independently 3–4kN (300-400kgf)	Generally considered the most useful for double-rope belaying
Air traffic controller, Bugs, and Variable controllers	Single or double: usually 2 x 9mm or similar	Slightly above most Stichts, can feed independently but has a tendency to 'jam' if feeding rope rapidly	Generally considered the most useful for double-rope belaying; good for abseils
Grigri and Single rope controller	Single rope, with a diameter of 10mm to 11mm. Note: It is unsafe to use Grigris on ropes of less than 10mm as the rope might slip.	If properly used, is suitable for sport belaying. Locks off automatically, helpful with inattentive/novice belayers. Tends to twist rope > 4kN (400 kgf).	Grigris 'lock off' rapidly and transfer excessive loads onto anchor points. Can 'drop' climbers seriously if they are incorrectly used.

Belaying Skills and Rope Management

Without doubt, if you climb much at all, you will one day rely totally on the 'safety chain' of preplaced protection, rope, slings, harnesses, knots, carabiners, belaying device and your partner. Often the weakest link is the human one, where inattention or a mistake in setting up belays can have tragic results.

Each belaying device has its advantages and disadvantages. Variants exist on most of the major types (*see* above), but all use the same principles:

Dynamic Rope Slippage

Most belay devices work on the principle of dynamic (planned) rope slippage. This allows for a gradual absorption of the energy of the falling climber into the system. There are two extremes of rope slippage:
1. When there is no or little slippage (e.g. in the Grigri). The rope is subjected to rapid and extreme tension, and all of the fall energy must be dissipated by rope stretch, harness and knot tightening, or by deformation of the climber's body.

2. When there is excessive slippage (for example when attempting to hold a long, serious fall). The rope pays out through the system too fast, causing 'rope burn' or worse to the belayer (with equally serious consequences for the falling climber).

As yet, no absolutely fail-safe system has been developed for long, serious falls. The ideal system would balance a certain amount of dynamic slippage with safe stopping power. Where long falls are expected or possible, the belayer could benefit from wearing supple leather gloves or similar protective handwear, archaic as this may at first appear!

BRAKING COEFFICIENT

This is the amount of force generated by the friction of the rope around/through the belay device or system. It varies according to rope diameter, age, type, angle of pull, and loading. It can be as high as 4kN (400kgf), where the belay system won't allow the rope to slip through it if strongly gripped, until the force exceeds 4kN.

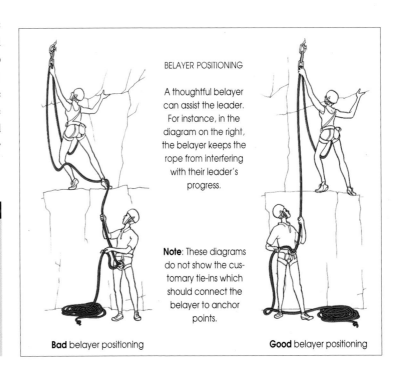

BELAYER POSITIONING

A thoughtful belayer can assist the leader. For instance, in the diagram on the right, the belayer keeps the rope from interfering with their leader's progress.

Note: These diagrams do not show the customary tie-ins which should connect the belayer to anchor points.

Bad belayer positioning

Good belayer positioning

Running belays (runners) are important! You should put in protection soon after leaving the stance.

Fall Factors

In any fall, most of the energy of the falling climber is dissipated by the rope. The greater the length of rope out, the more easily the energy is dissipated (a long piece of rope can stretch more and can absorb more energy via internal deformation).

The energy developed by a fall is proportional to the distance fallen. The longer the fall, the more energy needs to be absorbed by the system.

The ideal situation is to have a short fall at the top of a climb, with a lot of rope between the climber and the belayer. Any method of shortening the fall diminishes the risk. Running belays have the effect of shortening any fall. It is thus vital to place running belays as soon as possible after starting to climb.

Belaying is always of vital importance so avoid taking it casually – inattention can be fatal.

Right and opposite In situations like these, an alert belayer is vital!

'Fall factor' is the name given to the ratio between distance fallen and length of rope which is available to absorb the fall. For instance, a climber leaving a ledge falls after climbing 5m. He has 5m of rope to the belay device – falls this 5m, and then another 5m past the belay ledge, i.e. he falls 10m.

Fall factor = distance fallen ÷ rope out

His fall factor is thus 10m ÷ 5m = 2.

This (2) is the most serious fall factor.

Had he climbed up 3m, put in a running belay, climbed another 2m, then fallen, he would have fallen (in theory) 2m, then another 2m past the protection point.

Fall factor = 4m ÷ 5m = 0.8
– a much lower fall factor.

WHAT REALLY HAPPENS WHEN BRAKING A FALL

An 80kg climber falls from 10m above his belayer, and 10m past a belay point with no runners in:

He generates 80kg x 10m/s x 20m (*see* page 46) =16,000J (or N.m) of energy:

Fall factor = 20m of fall ÷ 10m of rope out = 2

At the end of the fall he has a velocity of 20m/s.

This must be arrested by rope elongation (20%) – some 3000J – leaving 13,000J to be absorbed somewhere else! About 1000J can be absorbed by the knot, climber's body, and movement of the belayer. The belay knot (if using a friction hitch) can lock only up to about 3000N of force if being tightly held by a moderately strong grip; then slippage starts. The rest is absorbed by rope slippage past the belay device – in the case of a friction hitch, this would require about 4m of rope slippage (12,000N.m/3000N). This would lead to a serious burn if the belayer had bare hands.

Actual distance fallen would be:

20m + 2m (stretch) + 4m (slippage) = 26m

CHAPTER FOUR

SPORT CLIMBING
The Rock Gymnast

The challenge of the vertical can be long and arduous, or short and arduous. In the world of sport climbing, the dedicated, limit-pushing climber strives to complete the 'hardest' route possible, irrespective of whether it is 4 or 400m long. Just as a sprint in athletics cannot be deemed 'less' of an achievement than a marathon because it demands a totally different yet equally taxing level of commitment, so sport climbing should not be viewed as either a lesser or a greater form of the art of climbing.

The essence of sport climbing lies in the preprepared nature of the route. A sport route has 'fixed' protection, i.e. the points into which climbers clip themselves are permanent structures, pre-placed in the rock. The only 'protection' equipment other than the rope usually consists of 'quickdraws', two carabiners joined by a short sling which are clipped into the *in situ* protection. Unlike in most other forms of climbing, it is considered normal to fall off a route repeatedly while trying to complete it.

Sport climbing is the most rapidly growing branch of climbing. Sport crags are usually easy to access, with no long walk-ins; the equipment required is less costly than a large traditional gear rack; there is a 'fun' element which

Quickdraws

appeals particularly to the younger generation; the competitive element is more visible; and the number of routes completed is generally greater and hence more satisfying in today's achievement-oriented world. Sport climbing is also inherently safer than other codes as the protection places are solid and reliable (it is important to take careful note of later

A long sport route in the Verdon Gorge, France.

Sport climbs are usually on steeply overhanging rock.

cautions though). From here, it is a small step to competition climbing, and hence to media hype, prizes, and the climbing 'big time'.

SPORT CLIMBING ETHICS

Falling off and repeating moves, resting on tight rope (allowing the belayer to 'hold' you), pulling on quickdraws during practice attempts, practising sequences of moves, inspecting the route on abseil or top-rope, watching others climb the route, asking for information, watching videos of the route, and even in extreme cases building 'models' of the route in one's training cellar – all of these are ethical and/or legitimate aspects of sport climbing.

CAUTION

Ropes are designed to deform and stretch on holding a fall. In the case of short falls of no more than 1m (3ft) or so (the most common falls in sport climbing), the deformation is usually temporary, and the molecules making up the individual monofibres reconform themselves if given sufficient 'rest' time. The recommended minimum is normally 15 to 20 minutes. If this time is not allowed for, the rope fibres will not be able to recover sufficiently and subsequent falls will soon start to rupture or break fibres irreversibly. This will weaken and 'age' the rope, and will eventually render it incapable of holding a serious fall.

Very few cases of rope breakage have ever been reported; however, another less serious – but also significant – consequence of rope ageing is the loss of elasticity. Reduced elasticity will cause ever-greater shock loading and stress on the climber, and all parts of the belay system.

Depending on whom you ask, you will get different answers as to what comprises 'acceptable practice'. There are, however, generally accepted mores and methods, and these are summarized below:

Types of Ascent

On-sight flash: this is considered by most to be the 'best style'. The climber walks up to a route and completes it from bottom to top on the first attempt, with no falls, 'dogging' or any preknowledge. He should not be given beta (information) in any form.

Flash: completing a route on one's first attempt, but with preknowledge. A small step below the on-sight flash, but still a highly regarded ascent.

Redpoint: the climber has practised the route any number of times and has worked out the critical holds and sequences. The redpoint is obtained when the climber finally completes the route from bottom to top with no falls or rests. Redpoint ascents are considered normal for the harder grades.

Pinkpoint: where the climber climbs as for a redpoint, but with all quickdraws preplaced. Many sport climbers no longer distinguish between redpoints and pinkpoints.

EQUIPMENT

The essentials are the same as for most types of climbing: boots, a rope, a harness, a screwgate carabiner, a belay device and some protection (*see* also page 78) in the event of falls when leading or top-roping.

Sport climbing may at first appear to require relatively unspecialized climbing gear, but there are many small but vital variations from the other branches of climbing.

THE ROPE

This is, generally speaking, a standard single dynamic kernmantel rope, from 10mm to 11mm, with 10.5mm being the most popular. Lengths are usually 50m (165ft), with 60m ropes becoming more common as longer routes (above 25m) are opened, particularly in Europe.

Specialized 'sport' ropes are coming into vogue, designed specifically to take into account the numerous short falls which are part of the game. Some are even differentially thickened, on the basis that, of a 50m rope, it is usually only the first 10m that takes severe stress in the belay device. Another trend is towards 9.5mm 'special' ropes for extreme sport routes; these ropes offer lightness while still possessing sufficient strength.

QUICKDRAWS

These consist of two carabiners joined by a short sewn sling. Many variations exist, but most climbers prefer one end to have a straightgate carabiner, which clips the bolt or peg, and the other a bentgate clipgate, which allows the rope to be clipped quickly and easily.

Quickdraw slings

HARNESSES

The trend is toward lightweight harnesses with fewer gear loops, as usually only a few quickdraws have to be clipped onto it. The Ultralightweight models are favoured by extreme climbers and for use in competitions. It becomes a personal compromise between comfort and weight.

CHALK BAGS

Considered essential in sport climbing, chalk bags are rapidly entering the domain of most types of rock climbing. Ensure that the bag has a good drawstring to prevent spillage. Size is a personal choice, but for serious sport climbing don't make it too big (excess weight) or too small (when you need chalk, you need it fast).

There are many varieties, but 'chalk' is basically 'light' magnesium carbonate – $MgCo_3.5H_20$ – or a similar form of magnesium carbonate which has a suitable 'water of crystallization' (the process in which water molecules are bonded into the crystal matrix, giving a substance its unique shape and properties). Chalk is used to dry the hands, thus enhancing grip. Years of observation have convinced many that its primary value is psychological. However, 'good' chalk does help, one way or the other.

ROCK BOOTS

'Real' sport climbers do not, and cannot, walk around in their boots. In order to maximize grip and sensitivity, sport climbers wear **tight** rock boots, usually at least two sizes smaller than their normal shoe size. 'Clunky' boots are no good for sport climbing.

Elasticized sides and pointed toes are painful but popular, as they allow the boot to be tight fitting yet still sensitive. Slip-on boots are fine if your feet are strong and used to the tensions of climbing, but they offer little support to beginners. Many boots now offer Velcro closures in place of laces – this is useful, but be aware that many of these 'softer' boots stretch with use, so sizing must be carefully watched.

BELAY DEVICES AND THE MAIN CARABINER

The carabiner used to belay with should be a screwgate or locking gate type in order to prevent it from accidentally opening.

Most belay devices (*see* page 58) are suitable for sport climbing, but remember that the belayer must expect frequent low-intensity falls, and may need to 'hold' the leader while he rests for extended periods of time. It is also essential to be able to 'feed' rope out quickly for the leader to clip the piece of protection, or to rapidly take it in again either after clipping or if the clip is 'missed'. Belaying with a friction hitch is thus not a good idea in sport climbing as it is difficult to reverse rope direction rapidly. A device which is popular with sport climbers is the Grigri – an auto-blocking device that works on a similar principle to the inertia reels of car safety belts.

These take practice to master, but are convenient for sport climbing, especially when the climber is belayed by a lighter person.

Air traffic controller (ATC) and auto-locking carabiner.

CAUTION

Grigris severely limit any rope slippage and thus can easily produce unacceptably high impact forces on protection points and climbers in the case of long falls. It is definitely **not** recommended to use Grigris for any other purpose than sport climbing on reliable anchor points, e.g. recently placed, solid, drilled bolt anchors.

A good number of climbers have been 'dropped' quite seriously by Grigris - the major reasons being incorrect loading (they load almost 'back to front', so take care **every** time), and belayers 'freezing' and holding back the release lever. Holding the rope on the incorrect (left) side during lowering can also jam the Grigri in an open configuration.

SPECIAL CLIMBING TECHNIQUES AND TRAINING

Many of the techniques shown below were developed in sport climbing and have quietly been adopted by the more traditional branches of climbing, helping to raise standards.

In sport climbing, one usually climbs on vertical to wildly overhanging rock, with significant 'slabby' sport climbs being restricted to a few areas like the Handegg slabs of Switzerland. Techniques thus focus on maximizing power and obtaining 'rests', on using cross-body tension or on efficient clipping of quickdraws.

The climbing techniques illustrated here are more specific to sport climbing. Other general techniques are discussed elsewhere.

Hanging on a straight arm while clipping in helps to conserve energy.

A twist lock on steep rock. The flagging right foot helps roll the body into the twist.

Twisting a lock off is a useful technique to help one achieve maximum reach.

This climber has used a drop knee and under cling to maximize reach. The opposing forces on her feet also allow a brief moment of 'rest'.

Far left Using a foot jam takes weight off the arms.

Left A high heel hook used to allow the left arm to move upwards.

By avoiding overreaching, the climber has the option of easily moving left or right.

The drop knee helps to achieve a lock off and keeps the climber close to the rock.

The left foot is 'flagging' – being used to assist balance rather than provide motion.

A left-hand closed crimp.

A deadpoint is a controlled lunge used to reach a distant hold.

Finger strength is needed to utilize small pockets in the rock.

A right-hand open crimp.

ENGRAMS

Technique training involves acquiring and reinforcing engrams – patterns of body movement which are registered in the brain. A good example is the engram for riding a bicycle; once mastered, you no longer have to consciously think about the individual processes. All that is required is to link up or combine patterns of previously stored movements such as 'turn left' or 'stop'.

Forming correct engrams right from the start is important, as bad technique learned early on is difficult to undo at a later stage.

Ways to help are:

• Learn techniques in 'safe' environments, e.g. bouldering, on a climbing wall or on a top-rope, where the fears of falling or sustaining injury are minimized. Technique does not develop easily on actual routes.

• Learn new techniques when fresh, not tired, as coordination goes awry when lactic acid has built up in your muscles.

• Once you have found a 'good' move or series of moves, repeat it several times as soon as you can to reinforce it. In gymnastics, many coaches will not accept a routine as 'bombproof' until it has been practised a thousand times!

• Regularly climb routes below your maximum grade, to achieve fluidity and enhance confidence. Stress inhibits engram development as you will revert to your most ingrained patterns of action. By training at your limit, you cannot develop new techniques, and can only reinforce the limited number of moves you are able to perform at that intensity.

• Work actively with friends or partners – this enables you to view new techniques and also obtain feedback on your own climbing style.

Once the engram has been 'programmed', then you can progressively push the patterning by attempting the move over and over again, until fatigued. In this way you will be able to use the technique when it is really needed.

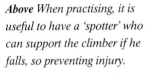

Above When practising, it is useful to have a 'spotter' who can support the climber if he falls, so preventing injury.

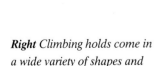

Right Climbing holds come in a wide variety of shapes and sizes. It is important for them to be 'tendon friendly'.

USEFUL TRAINING TIPS

• The best possible training for climbing is climbing. However, you will only achieve small improvements in your technique unless you vary your climbing, pushing yourself to the limits on some days, resting on others, and very often climbing 'just for fun'.

• Consider changing your focus. By concentrating on certain areas you can identify your weaknesses or even try to eliminate them. For instance, you could spend an entire training session just concentrating on the best use of your thumb, or the finger technique of one hand.

Work on your weaknesses. We often focus on our strong points, being too lazy or too embarrassed to admit our weaknesses. At first you might drop a grade or two if you are concentrating on precise foot placements to such an extent that you are losing out on your normal, secure hand grip. In the long term however, it will benefit you.

• Practise body positioning. A number of body orientations might get you through a particular move. However, some require less energy or effort than others. By trying the same move in a number of ways, you can learn which method works best. Once you have successfully completed a difficult move or sequence, don't just thankfully leave it – try it in another way.

• Deliberately change your style during training. If you are normally a powerful, aggressive climber, think 'light and fluid'; conversely, if you are a stealthy, steady climber, try moves in a 'bold and brutal' way, and so on.

• Vary your routines. In any one training session, you could try any number of ideas, such as speed climbing on routes or traverses, climbing using only one arm or one leg, climbing continuously at medium intensity for half an hour, climbing facing only in one direction, outside edging with your feet, climbing with 'no thumb', climbing blindfold, in slow motion, deliberately jerkily, and so on.

Apart from breaking the monotony of hours of climbing training in your home cellar or on the local bouldering wall, a varied programme will introduce many new techniques to your repertoire.

JERRY MOFFAT

Voted 'the most influential climber of the decade' in 1990 by the French magazine *Vertical*, Jerry Moffat was born in Leicester, UK, in 1963. He started climbing seriously at the age of 15 in Wales, and was soon repeating test pieces, such as Ron Fawcett's line Strawberries at Tremadoc. After moving to Sheffield, the forge of British climbing in the 1980s, he started to push British E6 with a series of his own hard routes. In 1982 he laid siege to the USA, repeating Genesis in Eldorado, and returned home with renewed vigour to establish climbs such as Revelations on Raven Tor and Masterclass and later Liquid Amber (E9, 7a), both at Pen Trwyn.

He gained instant fame both locally and internationally when he won the first International Climbing Competition to be held on British soil, stealing the title at Leeds from the reigning French climbers with a nail-biting climb.

Jerry is not the archetypal hard-training, clean-living cellar denizen. He revels in speed (a motorcycling accident put paid to climbing for a good while) and enjoys an active social life. Despite this, and what some might call his 'advanced years', he is still at the forefront of hard climbing around the world.

Left Jerry Moffat on Masters Edge, Sheffield, England.

Above On many types of rock, bolts are the only safe protection.

BOLTS AND THE SPORT CLIMBER

A 'bolt' in climbing terms is a piece of metal placed into a rock face to provide protection for climbers. Bolts are placed in predrilled holes and held in place permanently, either by an epoxy-resin glue or by a fitting on the bolt shaft that expands upon tightening. It is safe to say that, without bolts, there would be no such thing as sport climbing. Although climbing with preplaced (but removable) nuts, camming devices or pegs would serve the same purpose, it is seldom done. The very nature of sport routes – steep, strenuous, on overhangs or very blank rock – mitigates against the placing of other forms of protection. In addition, the ethos of sport climbing – unfettered movement over rock with the gymnastic element dominating – precludes the finicky placing of other 'gear'.

Thus, climbing on bolted routes becomes a joy – climb and clip, climb and clip. Great pleasure can be had in stunning surroundings, as on the long, multi-pitch bolted routes in many parts of Europe. One can climb fluidly and safely, yet still push oneself to physical and, on many routes, psychological limits.

Bolts, however, are still the source of a good deal of controversy; many climbers and nonclimbers consider bolting to be 'defacing the rock' or 'lowering the standard'. Bolt addicts argue that, without bolts, the standards of climbing would never have been so high, and that bolts allow otherwise impossible but elegant lines to be climbed. On the other hand, many bolt lines could be protected using natural gear, but are bolted for convenience.

One of the great recent controversies was the bolting of the first few hundred metres of the American Direct on the Petit Dru in the French Alps. It was argued that the guides wanted it for safe ascents (and retreats) for themselves and their clients. After many heated sessions between those who had bolted it and those who wished it to remain one of climbing's great challenges, most of the bolts have finally been removed.

One of the great early bolt controversies was over Cesare Maestri's 'bolt ladder' which enabled him to get up Cerro Torre in South America. The huge compressor he took up still hangs attached to cables, a memento of his epic but some contend questionable, feat (*see* page 16).

PLACING BOLTS

Bolts are generally placed on abseil or top-rope, using special battery-powered drills. In some areas, e.g. the big walls in Yosemite Valley, battery drills are outlawed and bolts have to be placed by the older, far more time-consuming method of hand drilling. This, the authorities argue, prevents the placing of superfluous bolts, as anyone who has placed bolts by hand would doubtless agree.

TECHNIQUES FOR BOLT PLACEMENT

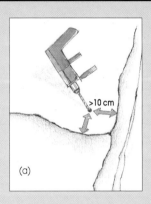

(a)

Expansion bolt

Bolt and hanger

• The rock should be checked for soundness by tapping firmly.

• Bolts should be placed at least 10mm (4in) away from edges (**a**) or from another bolt at top belay or lowering stations (**b**).

• The drill bit should be exactly the right size if using expansion bolts, as there is no room for error.

• The hole must be drilled at right angles to the rock (with certain glue-in 'looped' bolts the recommendation is to drill at a slight downward angle) and to the correct depth (**c**).

• A piece of tape around the drill bit (**d**) helps to keep this depth constant.

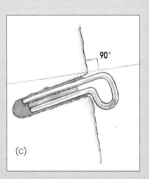

(c)

>10 cm

(b)

• The hole is then blown clean using a flexible pipe and, if possible, brushed out as well (rifle barrel-cleaning brushes work well or a defunct junior-size toothbrush).

• For glue-in anchors, the hole is then filled with the newly mixed epoxy from a suitable glue gun, and the anchor is inserted. Practice will allow you to use just enough glue to fill the hole but not to overflowing. Many bolters rub some rock dust into the epoxy at the surface interface to blend it with the rock.

• For straight (threaded) anchors, it is often recommended to spin the anchor slowly in the epoxy to create better adhesion. This can be done with a drill on a low speed. Too high a speed generates bubbles in the glue, weakening the bond.

• Glued anchors should be left unused for at least 12 hours before any kind of load is placed on them.

• Expansion bolts are placed in the hole with firm taps with a hammer, until just sufficient thread is showing. The hanger is then placed on the bolt and the nut is tightened. Beware of overdoing the torque as stainless steel bolts in particular can shear under extremely powerful fastening. The system is tight enough when tapping the hanger firmly results in no movement.

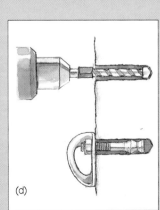

(d)

• Placing the hanger and nut on the bolt before tapping it in can help to seat the bolt properly, and also prevents accidental thread damage by the hammer.

• The stainless steel bolts of 10mm (0.4in) in diameter and 80mm (3.2in) or over in length, depending on the nature of the rock, are becoming recognized as the preferred standard for climbing bolts.

Above *By observing others one can improve one's technique.*

Above right *Bouldering is safer with an unobstructed landing.*

BOULDERING

This is mostly used for training, or pure fun, but many climbers also find it an end unto itself. Some of the modern 'boulder eliminates' are problems that need an incredible amount of power and determination, even though they might be only 3m (10ft) long and 0.5m (1.5ft) off the ground!

It is useful to carry a large chalk bag for long bouldering sessions and a mat to keep your climbing boots squeaky clean. Extremists have been known to carry in double-bed mattresses in order to soften uncomfortable landings!

Bouldering tends to be very sociable, and regular 'play-offs' add spice to the exercise. In addition, a companion who can 'spot' (break a fall by standing in the appropriate spot to catch you) is useful when tackling higher or awkwardly angled problems, or where the ground is uneven.

The most famous area for bouldering is Fontainebleau, south of Paris. However, great fun can be had on small rock outcrops, buildings, quarries or, of course, climbing walls.

Solo (unroped) rock climbing is bouldering taken to its extreme, and is definitely not for the faint-hearted or the inexperienced. Many regard it as the highest and purest form of the climbing art; others, emphasizing the risk element, regard it as incipient suicide. Certainly some first-rate climbers have met their end soloing, but there are also solo exponents who just seem to keep on going despite the alleged odds.

Risking the long arm of the law, some climbers do extensive solo 'buildering'. Everything from Nelson's Column to the Empire State Building has been climbed. Be aware of the double danger of this – the perils of falling not only off the building, but also foul of the law!

Right *The famous 'L'Eléphante' boulder in Fontainebleau, France.*

Above and left *The sport of buildering is an increasingly popular offshoot of more traditional bouldering.*

COMPETITION CLIMBING

The competitive urge is a common trait in mankind, and climbers have surely 'competed' ever since prehistory! Only recently has the competition element of climbing become formalized however, with the first major recognized event being held in Arco on the shores of Lake Garda, Italy, in 1985. This was held on 'pre-prepared' routes on the steep natural rock faces below the stunning setting of the ancient citadel. The 'defacing' of the rock in order to provide exactly the right grades caused havoc in the climbing community, and subsequent competitions worldwide have all been held only on artificial walls or in areas where the rock was not altered.

Competitions occur at all levels, from 'fun' events at local gyms and crags to huge international events, such as the Extreme Games in America, Serre Chevalier in France, the World Cup series or the perennial Arco Rockmasters invitation event.

Competition readiness entails being not only physically prepared, but mentally 'shatterproof'. A competitor's real battle is usually not with the wall, the route or his fellow climbers, but the pressures from within. Ways of overcoming the physical side have been discussed (see page 70), as the training is essentially the same, except that more time could be spent on the 'plastic' than on real rock.

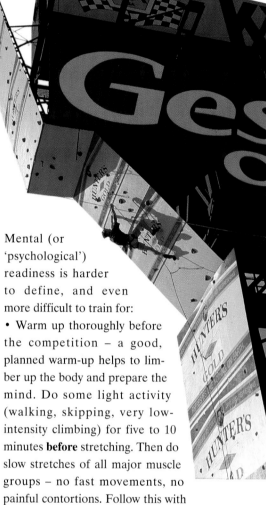

Mental (or 'psychological') readiness is harder to define, and even more difficult to train for:
• Warm up thoroughly before the competition – a good, planned warm-up helps to limber up the body and prepare the mind. Do some light activity (walking, skipping, very low-intensity climbing) for five to 10 minutes **before** stretching. Then do slow stretches of all major muscle groups – no fast movements, no painful contortions. Follow this with sets of moderately easy climbing or bouldering actions for 10 to 20 minutes. If possible, time it so your warm-up ends 10 to 15 minutes before you are due to enter the arena to climb.
• After the warm-up, stay warm. Put on some sort of jacket and trousers suited to the temperature – you want to be warm and supple, not hot and sweaty.
• When viewing the route (if this is allowed), focus on where you are going to clip the bolts from, and on the first few moves. Only then look ahead to how you are going to approach the more difficult sections. Just before leaving check the opening moves again, and run over these in your mind. The very act of starting well will help your confidence later.
• Spend some time quietly focusing on the positive aspects of the climb – what you liked about the route you viewed, which areas you feel confident about. Identify your goals – both realistic (perhaps not first

Right Competition climbing demands skill and immense concentration.

Below An artificial challenge against the breathtaking natural backdrop of Cape Town's Table Mountain, South Africa.

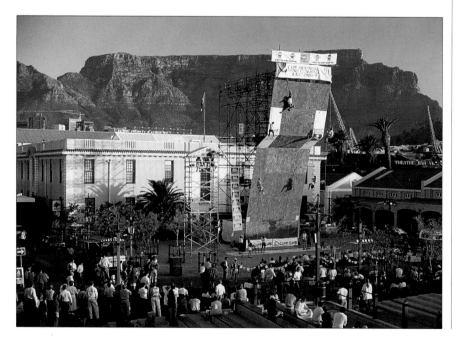

place, but 'one panel from the top', for example) and idealistic (standing on the winner's podium). Add some technical goals, such as 'I will remember to drop knee' or 'I will clip from a straight arm'.

• Do breathing exercises during your penultimate wait – slow your breathing down, breathe deeply but steadily. Your body will need the oxygen.

• Finally, check the chalk bag and the boots, walk out, spend a few seconds drawing that final deep breath, and climb. But don't forget to breathe – many climbers do!

Left A judge positioned to check the exact hold reached by the climber.

Bottom left Buoux in France is a sport climbing mecca.

Below Sport climbing on the steep granite of Tuolumne Meadows, California.

WHERE TO SPORT CLIMB

Most developed, and many undeveloped, countries boast sport routes. The mecca of sport climbing is still France, with thousands of routes in all grades, and ranging from 3m (10ft) to 300m (985ft) or longer.

Some 'must do's' include:

• The Verdon Gorge, near Castellane – scores of metres deep, with literally hundreds of bolted routes. Abseiling down to start one's route (the norm) is a mind-blowing experience. Grades from French 4 to 8.

• Buoux and Ceuse in central France – unforgettable, really steep climbs; mostly in the higher grades.

• The Calanques near Marseilles – sea-cliff climbing at its Mediterranean best in a range of grades.

• Finale Ligura, near the Italian-French border on the Mediterranean, and Arco at Lake Garda; both essentially 'hard man' areas but with some easier offerings at French grade 4 or 5.

• The Handegg and Grimsel Slabs in the Susten and Grimsel Passes, Switzerland – if your idea of sport climbing is long lead-outs at 'moderate' grades on friction slabs. (Taking a few trad-climbing nuts along reduces the long run-outs somewhat.)

Germany, England and America all have considerable numbers of sport climbs scattered around, mostly of the single-pitch variety. Other areas becoming increasingly popular are Spain and Australia, while even countries such as South Africa and Thailand have good sport climbing on offer.

CHAPTER FIVE

TRADITIONAL CLIMBING
The Mind Game

Leading on 'trad' equipment requires a cool head.

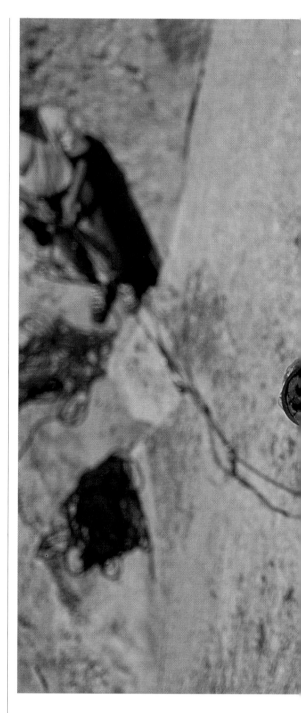

SPECIAL PROTECTION EQUIPMENT

The history of climbing development is closely linked to the advances in protection equipment and techniques. The enhanced methods of safeguarding the leader have led to the opening of new, previously inaccessible and often more difficult routes.

Equipment placed by leaders to safeguard both themselves and the other climbers is referred to as 'natural gear' or 'trad gear', as opposed to *in situ* bolts or pegs. This gear is usually placed by the leader and removed by the climbers following on for re-use on subsequent pitches or climbs.

In the early days, only a rope was used, and thus only the second climber was offered some protection in the event of a fall. The leader simply 'did not fall'! Some bolder, more innovative leaders took to untying from the rope, passing it behind a flake or bush, or through a hole, then tying on again. One can imagine the trepidation of the nervous second man who had to repeat this procedure. Slowly intermediate, or 'running', belays consisting of tied-off slings came to be accepted, with the art of one-handed knot tying being much in demand. Eventually carabiners, originating largely in military supplies after World War II, were used, making the clipping-in of the rope easier. It is hard for the modern, gadget-equipped leader to appreciate the boldness of these earlier pioneers.

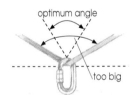

optimum angle

too big

USING A SLING
When it is used as an anchor,
the smaller the angle at the
bottom of the sling the better.
It should preferably be less
than 60 degrees.

The Needles in California is a trad climber's paradise of crack-rich granite spires.

Sewn sling

SLINGS

Useful for draping around flakes or spikes, or threading through chockstones or holes, slings are also invaluable in extending other forms of protection. They tend to be made from flat or tubular tape, and sewn slings, which do away with bulky and less secure knots, are now common. Tape knots are notorious for working loose, even when done correctly, and should be thoroughly and frequently checked. Knots also reduce the strength of the tape by as much as 50%.

Slings are vulnerable to abrasion on sharp edges, and the sides of the sling in particular should be carefully checked as some slings come with a 'locking stitch' down one edge – once this is abraded, the entire cross-fibre network of the sling can easily unravel, drastically reducing strength. When using slings round trees, bushes or columns, it is advisable to put them as low as possible in order to reduce leverage. Always beware of trees, no matter how solid they look, as branches can be rotten and some large trees are surprisingly shallow rooted.

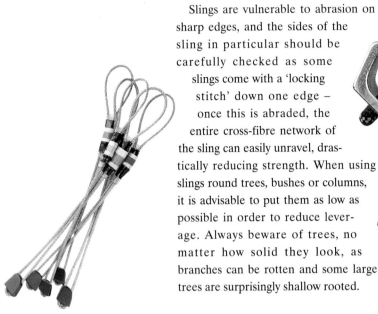

Hexentrics

A set of micro-nuts

PEGS AND WEDGES

Metal pegs and wooden wedges made their appearance in the Dolomites of Europe during the years between the World Wars; variations of these are still the stock in trade of many aid climbers. A wide range of sizes and types exists, from minute RURPs ('realized ultimate reality pitons') to huge bongs (*see* Chapter Six on Aid Climbing).

Old *in situ* pegs are still commonly found in the Alps and Dolomites. Care must be taken in using these as many date from as early as the 1950s or before. A solid-looking exterior can hide a rusted or ill-placed base. The peg should be tested by tapping it with a hammer and watching for movement as well as listening to the sound. A clear high ring usually indicates that it is solid.

NUTS OR 'CHOCKS'

Chockstones wedged in cracks had been used from early times, but legend has it that the first metal chockstones were nuts 'borrowed'(!) from the Llanberis railway line up Snowdon in Wales. Climbers tied the nuts off on bits of rope and stuck them in suitable cracks and wedges.

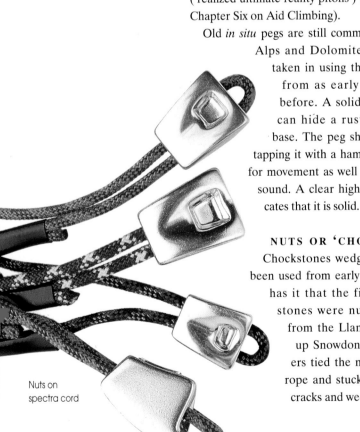

Nuts on spectra cord

In the 1960s, purpose-designed nuts were produced, such as the famous hexes and hexentrics and the moac wedges. These have largely been superseded by hi-tech composite aluminium, computer-designed nuts, although the old favourites are still popular with many climbers.

Nuts can be found on standard rope or tape, on special high-tensile nylon cord (spectra) or on swaged wire (*see* glossary). Most are tapered in such a way that they lodge in a variety of crack shapes and sizes, and vary from micro-nuts for tiny cracks to huge aluminium wedges, e.g. the hexentric 11. Breaking strains vary from about 2.5kN (50kgf) to over 10kN (100kgf). Some nuts, such as hexentrics and tri-cams, have a camming action, which pulls them tighter as the load increases. The most secure placements are obtained by carefully selecting the best orientation for nuts and wedges.

Removing nuts can be a problem, especially if the leader has given them a strong tug to lodge them. A nut-remover (or picker) on both the leader and second's rack is invaluable in preventing skinned knuckles.

Nut pickers (the top one has prongs to assist in removing friends)

ACTIVE CAMMING DEVICES

A revolutionary development occurred in the late 1970s with the invention of active camming devices (ACDs), also called spring-loaded camming devices (SLCDs). Designed to enable the placement of protection in the long, mildly flaring cracks of the Yosemite Valley, ACDs altered forever the nature of protection. Space-age technology has led to a reduction in weight and an increase in the number of available sizes which now range from as little as 10mm (0.4in) to almost 200mm (7.8in). There are few crack situations where a leader is unable to place protection these days.

Three-cam devices allow for thinner or narrower placements, although they do tend to be less stable than the four-cam option. Spring-loaded opposed wedges (e.g. the Rock 'n Roller) can work in tiny, near-vertical, parallel-sided cracks.

Great care must be taken in placing these to prevent over- or undercamming, and to ensure that all

Flexible and solid stemmed ACDs

of the cams are in contact with the rock. Loose cams increase the tendency of ACDs to 'walk' into cracks, which can in turn reduce their holding power or make them difficult to extract.

ACDs often seem to worm their way into narrow cracks, so a useful tip is to attach thin accessory cords to the trigger bars to aid removal. Many nut pickers have curved hooks to overcome this. Older model Friends have a solid stem. If not placed deep enough in a horizontal crack, this stem could break in holding a fall. Often a 4mm (0.15in) cord through the first hole in the trigger bar is used as a back-up.

All ACDs need to be cleaned periodically to allow for smooth camming action (warm water and mild soap will do). The cam units must then be sprayed with a silicone lubricant. As with ropes, avoid using oil or grease.

Remember: ACDs only work to full specification if used correctly. Don't blame the device if your poor placement fails as a result of overcamming, undercamming or incorrect sizing.

Camalots

THE BIRTH OF ACDS

Ray Jardine designed the Friend – the first active camming device – to allow his group to climb the previously poorly protected Yosemite cracks in safety. He was motivated by the fact that the group couldn't constantly afford to buy new pegs, so some form of easily placeable and removable protection was urgently required. The next (and perhaps apocryphal) part of the story came a few years later when Jardine jokingly remarked of a desperate, unclimbed off-width crack: 'I'll lead that with a number 17 Friend!' (The largest size at the time, about 8cm (3in) wide, was a number 4.) The next weekend his proud (and perhaps sadistic) workers presented him with... a 'number 17 Friend'. Jardine had no choice – he led the crack, and survived!

Friends come in a wide range of sizes.

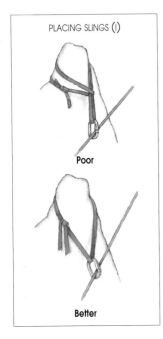

PLACING SLINGS (I)

Poor

Better

THE PLACEMENT OF NATURAL GEAR

There is no substitute for experience or practice. For the beginner or even the 'rusty' oldster, a few hours of practice at placing gear just off ground level will bear dividends at more serious altitudes. Many innovative ways can be found to place nuts, slings and ACDs and only practice will ensure quick, secure placements. A good exercise for novice leaders is to find an area close to ground where there are many different possible placements, and engage in a game of 'gear placing' with a companion: each tries to put in as many 'bombproof' placements as they can, within a time limit, using one hand, and so on.

PLACING SLINGS

A sling can be draped around a tree or through a wormhole. However, avoid using Lark's foot configurations where possible, as these can weaken the sling by up to 75%!

If hooked over a flake or knob of rock, the use of a heavy carabiner or some other form of additional weight is advised; this prevents the sling from being hooked loose as the leader continues climbing.

If slings are being used to connect two or three anchor points, there are certain principles that prevent the failure of one point causing subsequent failure of the whole belay point.

PLACING SLINGS (II)

A self-equalizing anchor. Note the twists in the sling.

Correct

The 'dangerous triangle'

Incorrect

A useful way of tying off a lot of anchor points to obtain equal loading is through the use of a **cordelette**. This long cord is tied off to suit the situation.

Right Choosing the best size of protection comes with experience.

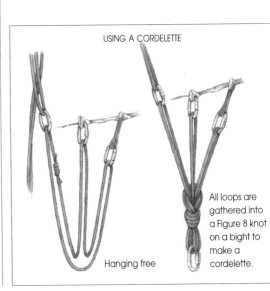

USING A CORDELETTE

All loops are gathered into a Figure 8 knot on a bight to make a cordelette.

Hanging free

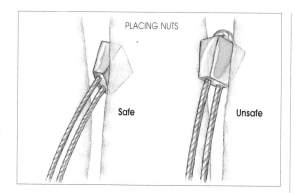

PLACING NUTS

Safe   Unsafe

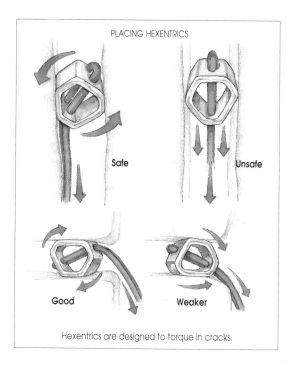

PLACING HEXENTRICS

Safe   Unsafe

Good   Weaker

Hexentrics are designed to torque in cracks.

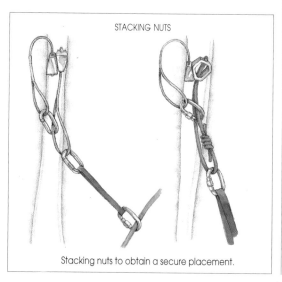

STACKING NUTS

Stacking nuts to obtain a secure placement.

Left Cracks lend themselves to the use of traditional gear.

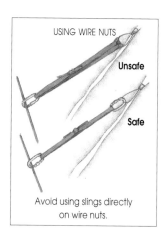

USING WIRE NUTS

Unsafe

Safe

Avoid using slings directly on wire nuts.

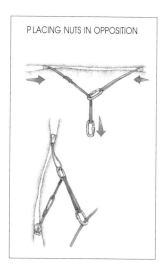

PLACING NUTS IN OPPOSITION

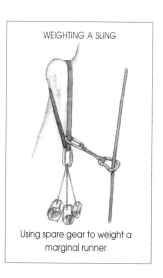

WEIGHTING A SLING

Using spare gear to weight a marginal runner

PLACING NUTS

Many climbers carry their nuts clipped in bunches of related size on a single carabiner. This allows for quick reselection of another size if you do not choose the right one first time. The nut is then placed, clipped off from the bunch, and a carabiner and sling or quickdraw clipped to the nut. Avoid clipping the rope directly into the carabiner clipped to the nut as it is more likely to dislodge the nut; there is also the danger that the rope can cross the gate and unclip from the carabiner.

The nut should be lodged tight with a firm tug on the sling. (Make sure that your second has a nut-removing tool as trying to remove a well-placed nut could become a frustrating and expensive exercise.) If it appears that the nut might slide out as the leader moves past, consider weighting it in a similar way to a sling (*see* illustration, right).

Placing nuts in opposition can be useful for preventing movement of the key placement.

Right and opposite Good
ACD placement is vital
for climbing safety and
peace of mind.

PLACING FRIENDS AND OTHER SPRING-LOADED CAMMING DEVICES (ACDs)

These rely on solid contact between all of the cams and the rock. Although marginal placements can be obtained in flaring cracks, ACDs are designed to work in parallel-sided situations or very mild flares.

ACDs should be orientated so that the axle is pointing in the direction of the expected load, otherwise they might twist out of the optimal position on loading. Both overcamming and undercamming is dangerous, as the gear cannot 'bite into' the rock on loading as it was designed to.

In ACDs with a solid stem, try to place them deep so that the stem cannot be bent over the edge. If this will cause problems in removal, then tie off the stem with accessory cord close to the cams as a back-up. Many ACDs operate better in one orientation than another, with the narrower cams facing in a particular direction. Experiment with this to improve the placement.

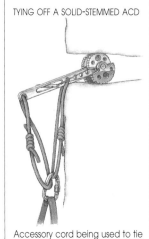

TYING OFF A SOLID-STEMMED ACD

Accessory cord being used to tie off a solid-stemmed ACD in case of a stem breaking.

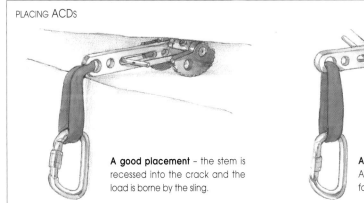

PLACING ACDs

A good placement – the stem is recessed into the crack and the load is borne by the sling.

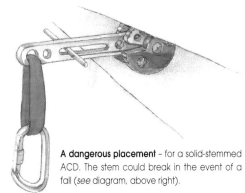

A dangerous placement – for a solid-stemmed ACD. The stem could break in the event of a fall (*see* diagram, above right).

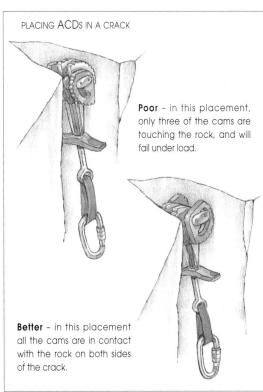

PLACING ACDs IN A CRACK

Poor – in this placement, only three of the cams are touching the rock, and will fail under load.

Better – in this placement all the cams are in contact with the rock on both sides of the crack.

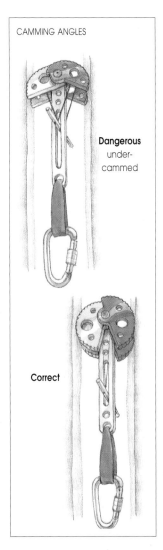

CAMMING ANGLES

Dangerous under-cammed

Correct

EXTENDING RUNNERS AND SINGLE AND DOUBLE ROPE TECHNIQUES

If climbing with a single rope, one has to be careful to ensuring that runners are long enough to prevent the rope 'zigzagging'. This can lead to gear being pulled out in a fall. Climbing on a twin rope gives one more options, as alternate runners can be placed on either rope or only one rope can be clipped to a set of runners if moving sideways.

A belayer correctly tied on to cope with upward or downward shock. Note that the leader has placed runners as soon as possible to diminish the fall factor.

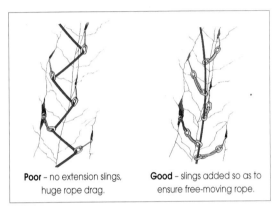

Poor – no extension slings, huge rope drag.

Good – slings added so as to ensure free-moving rope.

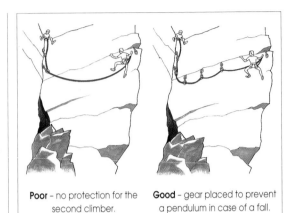

Poor – no protection for the second climber.

Good – gear placed to prevent a pendulum in case of a fall.

THE LEADER'S RESPONSIBILITIES

Although many climbers climb as an 'equal pair' and the responsibilities are then fully shared, in many cases the 'leader' is the only experienced climber. All points apply equally to partners of equivalent experience climbing together.

Before beginning the climb, the leader of the party or of the pitch in question is ultimately responsible for checking that he is correctly on belay and that all knots and belay anchors are sound and appropriately connected. In fact, using a 'buddy system' of constantly cross-checking (as is common with scuba divers) is an excellent fail-safe method that is, sadly, seldom used in climbing. It is far too common to take belaying lightly, and for the leader to wander up the rock without ensuring that the second man really knows what to do in the event of a fall or even that he is truly being belayed.

Be aware too of properly protecting the second on traverses, particularly if climbing as a party of three with two ropes – what could be an inconvenient fall for a leader could be fatal for those following.

The leader should always let someone know the intended destination and expected time of return. In addition, he should ensure that every member of his party knows the intended route, any 'escape' routes, the descent details, and that they are properly equipped to deal with weather and any exigencies of the climb, including the possibility of the leader falling and injuring himself severely.

Some preliminary preparation with inexperienced climbers will be both of interest and value to them. Each climber should know the essential knots, how to belay, and what to do in case of an emergency.

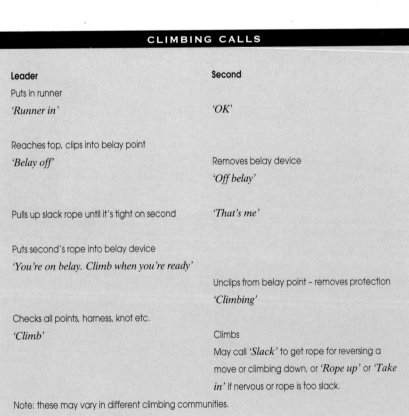

CLIMBING CALLS

Leader	Second
Puts in runner	
'Runner in'	'OK'
Reaches top, clips into belay point	
'Belay off'	Removes belay device
	'Off belay'
Pulls up slack rope until it's tight on second	'That's me'
Puts second's rope into belay device	
'You're on belay. Climb when you're ready'	
	Unclips from belay point – removes protection
	'Climbing'
Checks all points, harness, knot etc.	Climbs
'Climb'	May call 'Slack' to get rope for reversing a move or climbing down, or 'Rope up' or 'Take in' if nervous or rope is too slack.

Note: these may vary in different climbing communities.

JOE BROWN

An almost mythical name in world climbing, Joe Brown is one of the true masters of the art. The youngest in a family of seven, his childhood was spent working in the Manchester slums after his father died when he was 12. The same year, he started climbing, completely un-tutored, with some friends and at 16 he was climbing the great gritstone routes of Sheffield. Trips to Wales and Scotland followed and by the age of 18 he was ready to begin his record of great ascents.

Hundreds of routes have fallen to Joe Brown, most done with his partner, Don Whillans. Many feel that modern rock climbing owes its existence to this pair, who pushed the limits way beyond the boundaries of the day. Brown perfected 'pebble protection' – carrying stones in his balaclava, he would jam these into cracks with the rope threaded behind them.

His record ascents of the West Face of the Dru with Whillans in 1953, the Aiguille du Blaitière via what is now known as the 'Fissure Brown' in 1954, and the Mustagh Tower in the Karakorum in 1955 reveal the alpine and big wall sides of this unpretentious climber. Equally at home on Scottish ice and gritstone, Brown has climbed routes that often stayed unrepeated for many years.

Left Cenotaph Corner, Wales; Joe Brown spurred rock climbing to new heights when he finally ascended this open-book corner-crack in 1950.

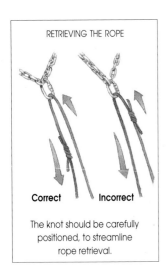

Correct   **Incorrect**

The knot should be carefully positioned, to streamline rope retrieval.

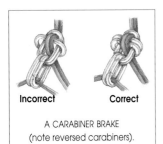

Incorrect   Correct

A CARABINER BRAKE
(note reversed carabiners).

ABSEILING

Descending the rope (called abseiling or rappeling) is often the safest and easiest way to the bottom of the crag. It is also a useful means of escaping from a crag in bad weather.

The Classic Abseil

This is seldom used these days, but might become necessary in unusual situations. The rope (usually doubled so that it can be pulled down from the bottom) is passed between the legs from the front, round the back and forwards over the hip, and then hitched over the shoulder from front to back on the opposite side. Without padding on the thigh and neck, it is excruciatingly painful to perform.

Friction Hitch (see page 57)

This works well but twists the rope (especially doubled ropes). The harness carabiner also heats up considerably.

Friction hitches should always be used with a large locking carabiner. The direction of the gate is important to prevent the rope running on the gate and possibly forcing it open.

Belay Plates (see page 59)

These work smoothly and well, but do cause both the harness carabiner and the plate to heat up on long abseils. Advantages are that they keep the ropes separate (useful for pulling down) and do not twist the ropes.

Figure 8 Descendeurs (see page 59)

These were designed with abseiling in mind, and are probably the best option. Their large size enables them to dissipate heat and keeps the heat away from the harness carabiner. Depending on whether the device is loaded from the 'top' or the 'bottom', slightly differing amounts of friction are generated.

Figure 8s do have certain disadvantages: they tend to twist the rope and it is quite easy to 'lock' the rope accidentally in a Lark's foot if one passes over an edge (a common and frustrating occurrence, for

Right A good, relaxed abseil stance is important. Keep feet apart to aid balance.

A TRADITIONAL 'CLASSIC' ABSEIL

(note the padded jacket).

beginners in particular). Some devices have 'wings' or are angled to prevent this from happening.

Carabiner Brakes
(see illustration far left)

These are effective, and by 'stacking' sets more friction can be generated – useful in rescues or when abseiling with a heavy load. A carabiner brake can also be used in addition to a belay plate, etc., in order to increase friction. Screwgates are preferred to clipgates, and straightgates are preferred to bentgates.

Grigris (see page 61)

A Grigri can be used on a single rope and is an effective abseil device which also allows the climber to stop in order to remove or place gear. Grigris do not work well on old, worn ropes with patches of varying thickness, and can 'jump' down rapidly over the different thicknesses before gripping again. Take care.

Special Devices

Devices such as the rack, Petzl stop or carabiner bar are used largely in rescue situations, caving or long, planned abseils. However, these devices are rather specialized and are best dealt with in the context of these activities.

GENERAL ABSEIL PRINCIPLES

Superfast long abseils look good in action movies and can be fun. They do, however, play havoc with ropes and other equipment; the heat generated when trying to stop can actually melt the rope.

Take abseils slowly and gradually. Jumping out from the rock or abseiling jerkily causes the rope to elongate cyclically, and this can abrade the rope on rock edges, or even loosen top anchor points.

Keep your feet in contact with the rock when possible, and adopt a 'horizontal' stance with your feet level with your hips.

Tying a knot in the rope ends, or tying them together in the case of double ropes, prevents you from accidentally abseiling off the end of the rope on multipitch descents.

RETRIEVING THE ROPE

To remember which is the correct rope to pull on in a double-rope abseil, as well as to keep the ropes separated for easier retrieval, clip a carabiner onto the rope and then attach this via a sling to your harness prior to abseiling. The 'pull down' rope is then the one which keeps the knot on the lower side of the abseil anchor (illustrated top right).

By taking care on the setup, problems can be avoided. It often helps to set the knot past an edge at the top, even if the last man has to then clip on to his abseil device and climb down to below the edge before starting the abseil.

Beware of dislodged rocks or debris when pulling ropes. A steady pull is better than a series of jerks, as the rope ends are less likely to fly around and catch on something. Inevitably, one day a rope will jam. If all desperate attempts to flick it loose fail, then one climber will have to climb back up, belayed by whatever rope is available until he or she can prusik (*see* page 92) up both ropes once both ends are reachable. When prusiking, it is advisable to tie on at intervals with figure 8 knots in case of a prusik failure.

SAFEGUARDING ABSEILS

Stacking: one leader with a few inexperienced climbers can attach the rest of his party to the rope in a 'stack' before abseiling himself. This enables him to call them down one-by-one, while he safeguards them by holding the bottom of the rope.

A STACKED ABSEIL

This can be used to allow a number of inexperienced climbers to evacuate a ledge safeguarded by the leader from below. It is important to ensure that all anchors are solid.

Prusik knots: by attaching a prusik to the ropes and the climber, the abseiling climber is protected if he lets go of the rope. The knot is usually placed below the belay device and tied off to a leg-loop on the harness. It is held open with the braking hand, and will lock automatically if released. The French prusik is usually used as it releases easily under load if required.

Shunts: the Petzl shunt is useful for protecting abseils, and allows for safe prolonged stops should the need arise (*see* lever cam devices, page 93).

ROPE RETRIEVAL

The carabiner and sling are used to both keep the ropes from twisting, and to identify the correct rope to pull down after the abseil.

SPECIAL ABSEILING TECHNIQUES

Multipitch abseils often require good planning to ensure speed of descent. Send one party member down with the needed protection gear on a single rope, protected on the second rope. They can then fix the next point, ensure that both ropes are down, and pull in the next person if they have had to negotiate an overhang (remember to start your 'swing in' by pushing off in small jumps before going over the overhang). Tie rope ends off to the next anchor point on multipitch abseils in case of top anchor failure.

Diagonal abseils can be difficult. It often causes less wear and tear on the rope if all but the last climber abseil straight down on one rope until level with the target ledge and then climb sideways to it, with the second rope acting as a belay from above. The last climber must then abseil down both ropes and pendulum (swing) in to the target ledge. This has the advantage that the rope is only abraded once.

Abseiling with a heavy pack can flick the climber over. There are two solutions:
• wear some sort of chest-harness or sling
• suspend the pack below you directly from the abseil carabiner.

Marginal abseil points: if the top anchors are not very secure, the last person can use their body weight to help anchor the abseil rope. It is often best for them to sit down, preferably braced behind a rock. The first climber to abseil can place protection on the way down, which might help to hold a fall should the top anchors give way. They then place secure anchors at the bottom of the abseil. The last person has to abseil down gingerly, removing the safety runners as they go. They should be backed up with a prusik or shunt on both ropes, with a carabiner clipped onto one rope and their harness, in order to avoid going off the top of the rope should the top anchor fail and the prusik be ripped down because of slippage.

Above An abseil away from the rock. The abseiler is protected with a prusik loop.

Opposite On popular routes, such as the Dent Geant in the Mont Blanc range, abseils need to be done efficiently in order to prevent congestion.

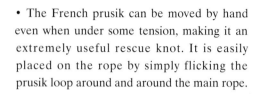

ASCENDING THE ROPE

It is vital to know these techniques for emergency reasons or to save time on long routes where mechanical ascenders such as jumars are used by seconding climbers. In all cases it is best to practise using these knots and ascenders somewhere in comfort and safety – halfway up the Eiger in a snowstorm is not the place to learn prusik techniques!

In general, one should clip slings from both foot and harness ascenders to the harness for safety. By carefully adjusting the length of footloops, one can arrive at the optimal configuration for comfort combined with minimal energy use. Use the feet for upward motion rather than the hands. In all rope ascents try to move upwards smoothly, without 'bouncing'. The rope often runs over edges, and the continuous up-and-down movement could easily abrade it.

In extremis, many ways of ascending the rope can be tried, ranging from a James Bond-type use of shoelaces as prusiks, to using slings or clove-hitch knots for standing on if you only have one prusik loop. Necessity is the mother of invention.

Petzl shunt

THE ESSENTIAL KNOTS

Karl Prusik, an Austrian climber, developed the first commonly recognized knot for ascending ropes. Many variations exist on the basic theme which consists of winding a thinner rope around a thicker one until sufficient friction is generated to prevent the loaded thin rope from sliding. These loops are universally referred to as prusik loops.

Commonly used are the standard prusik knot, the klemheist, the bachman knot and the French prusik.

• The standard prusik knot uses less rope than the other three, but jams under load.

• The klemheist can be used with tape slings as well as with thin rope slings.

• The bachman knot incorporates a carabiner, which gives a 'handle' to pull up on when ascending. It is good on wet or icy ropes.

Opposite Felicity Butler stays focused on Anxiety Neurosis, Mount Arapiles, Australia.

Below Long jumars can be tiring with a pack. Clip the pack directly to the lower jumar, or haul separately.

• The French prusik can be moved by hand even when under some tension, making it an extremely useful rescue knot. It is easily placed on the rope by simply flicking the prusik loop around and around the main rope.

Ascending

The top loop is clipped to the harness; the bottom loop is extended to allow one's foot to stand in it. By moving the bottom loop higher and standing on it, one can move the top loop upwards and then sit back on it, and so on.

Prusiks have been known to slip! If this becomes a long slip, they might fail as a result of friction melting the loop. To prevent problems on a long prusik, tie knots at intervals in the rope below and attach these to a spare carabiner clipped to the harness via clove hitches or figure 8 knots.

MECHANICAL ASCENDERS

Often called 'jugs' by climbers, a variety of these exist. All grip onto the rope when loaded either by a set of one-way teeth or by a camming action which traps the rope. Many mechanical ascenders have good safety catches built in to prevent accidental disengaging from the rope (a problem in earlier models).

Jumars: the first popular commercial ascenders. They make use of angled teeth and can have comfortable handles for convenience. With matched 'right- and left-hand' pairs, jumars allow fast ascents if one has the length of foot and the body loops correctly adjusted.

Jumar

They do not work too well on frozen or icy ropes however, and tend to clog up in muddy or icy conditions. The teeth also damage the rope sheath if used extensively. A number of significant variants exist, but the principle is the same.

Remember never to push a jumar hard up against a knot, as it has to be fractionally unloaded before it can be released.

Lever cam devices: the most common of these is the petzl shunt, but once again other variants exist. These do not cut into the rope sheath and usually lock well on wet and mildly iced-up ropes. They are also easier to move down in order to descend the rope as there are no teeth to catch. The shunt can also be used to ascend a double rope.

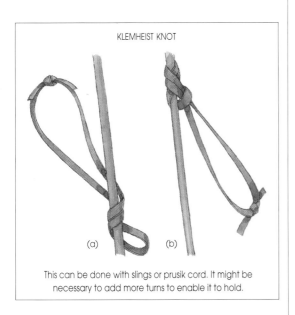

KLEMHEIST KNOT

(a)   (b)

This can be done with slings or prusik cord. It might be necessary to add more turns to enable it to hold.

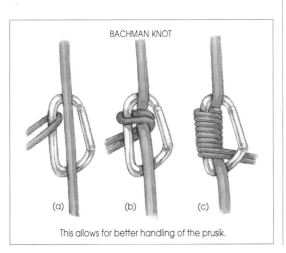

BACHMAN KNOT

(a)   (b)   (c)

This allows for better handling of the prusik.

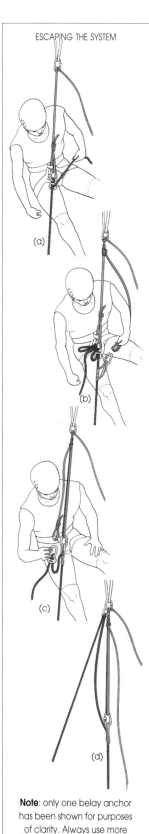

(a)

(b)

(c)

(d)

Note: only one belay anchor has been shown for purposes of clarity. Always use more than one anchor.

EMERGENCY PROCEDURES

Climbing always contains some degree of risk. Being prepared to cope with emergency situations which may, with any luck, never occur, is a vital component of training for climbing. Emergency situations are always unique and a combination of improvisation and trained readiness is essential to finding a solution to your particular problem.

PROBLEMS WITH THE SECOND CLIMBER

For many who work with inexperienced climbers or those less able than themselves, this is a real possibility. Out of sight, somewhere down there on the traverse, four pitches up, comes the voice: 'I can't do this move. Help.' What can you do?

Various options present themselves:

• Tie the climber off, then abseil down and help them across.

• Haul on the rope, pulling the climber up to you.

• Cut the rope and go away…!

In the final analysis, whatever your decision, there is always a solution if you have the skills and the time to employ them.

Escaping from the System

A belayer, be it leader or second, may need to remove himself from the belay chain in order to render assistance to a fallen or stuck climber.

The basic method (illustrated left) is:

• Lock off the belay device (a).

• Attach a prusik or locking device to the rope going

to the climber; a French prusik is best as it can be later released even under load (b).

• Tie the prusik or locking device to the anchor points via a sling or, if you do not have one, a loop of rope. If you are using your rope, think about what you are going to have to do with it next – will it be best to use the far end, the end nearest to the climber or somewhere in the middle? Don't just do, PLAN!

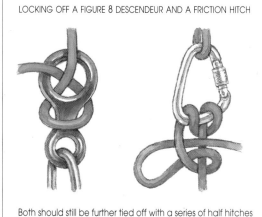

LOCKING OFF A FIGURE 8 DESCENDEUR AND A FRICTION HITCH

Both should still be further tied off with a series of half hitches around the body of the descendeur, or the rope.

• Tie a back-up clove-hitch knot (c), or a locked-off friction hitch (for easy release later) in the stricken climber's rope and attach it to the anchors. The loop must be long enough to ensure that it does not tighten up when the load is transferred to the prusik.

• Slowly release the belay hand, transferring load onto the prusik. Check that it is holding.

• You (the belayer) can then remove the belay device and release yourself from the situation.

Part of the rope is now free for use to get down to the climber via abseil, or to arrange a hoisting or lowering system (d).

For lowering, the locked-off friction hitch is already in place; all that you have to do is nudge the French prusik until it releases. Remember of course to hold the 'live' rope or the injured climber will plummet downwards!

Hoisting

Assisted hoist: the simplest hoist. It can be used if the victim is less than 1/3 rope length below the rescuer, conscious and able to reach the lowered rope. If the problem is a simple one, then the belayer does not even have to escape the system, but can simply put on a safety locking prusik below the belay device.

A bight (loop) of rope is then passed down to the victim with a locking carabiner on it. This is attached to the victim's harness, and the victim and belayer together hoist upwards.

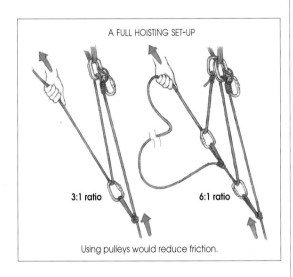

A FULL HOISTING SET-UP

3:1 ratio   6:1 ratio

Using pulleys would reduce friction.

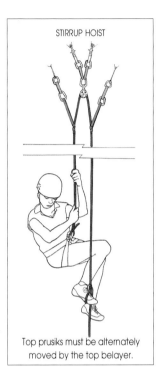

STIRRUP HOIST

Top prusiks must be alternately moved by the top belayer.

Stirrup hoist: used where ½ the length of the rope is concerned, or the full length in the case of double ropes. The victim uses one rope (tied off or placed on a prusik) for his foot prusik loop, and the other rope becomes the haul and belay rope from above.

If the victim has no prusik loop, then the 'foot' rope has a loop tied in the end, and it is 'hauled' alternately from above. By using one rope over a pulley, he can effectively hoist himself up, providing the top prusik points are controlled (*see* diagram top right). This method causes significant rope stretch.

Full hoist: (illustrated above) this is used when the victim cannot assist the rescuer. It is not easy as friction, even if only over carabiners, reduces efficiency.

It is vital to practise setting up these hoists as they can become quite complicated on a small ledge.

Fallen Leader

If the leader is hanging way above you, the only option is to tie him off, then prusik up to the anchor point above him.

To get down to him if hauling is impossible,

rearrange the prusiks and then prusik down the rope. It is then possible to tend to his injuries as best you can, as well as to retrieve some leading gear to back up anchor points.

If two ropes are being used, the process of abseiling for help or hauling the leader onto a ledge is simplified as you can use the other rope as a 'slack rope' on which to abseil down to the leader.

You can then untie (or cut) this rope from the leader, prusik back up to the high point, add some extra protection gear if possible, and abseil off to the belay ledge.

From there you can either haul the leader in when lowering him or abseil down, past the leader, using the spare rope, and pick him up on the way (if necessary by now cutting his other rope).

RESCUE TIPS

• Often going down is easier than going up, even if you are one pitch from the end of a 10-pitch route.
• If abseiling with a second person or heavy bag attached, use carabiner brakes above the abseil device to increase the friction afforded by normal abseil devices.
• An often overlooked solution is to cut a rope – either to create extra slings or to release someone from a desperate situation. (One should naturally make sure that they are fastened to something else first!)
• In self-rescues, back-up, back-up, back-up. Check each link in the safety chain carefully before doing anything. Safety is more vital than speed.

Top Climbers should be able to handle emergency situations, particularly in remote areas such as the Cedarberg mountains.

Opposite *An experienced leader helping a novice on a traverse.*

CHAPTER SIX

BIG WALL AND AID CLIMBING

Life on the Vertical

*Big wall climbing is
characterized by the need
for large amounts of gear.*

In today's mountaineering, the terms 'big wall' and 'aid' or 'artificial' climbing often tend to be associated, although historically they evolved differently.

Aid climbing is the technique of using some sort of equipment placed in the rock to hold the climber's weight as he ascends. It can be as basic as pulling on a piece of protection to assist one over a difficult move or as complex as doing an entire route on specialized pieces of gear or bolts, without any free climbing. Aid climbing is presently used for ascending currently 'unfreeable' routes or to give increased speed in alpine situations, or in the case of an emergency.

In **free climbing** the rope or pieces of gear are not used for upward motion – this would be considered 'bad style'. Top climbers are presently free climbing routes which were once 'aid-able only'; however, there will surely always be a route that can only be overcome with points of aid.

From the earliest of Alpine climbs, climbers have used pieces of gear for pulling or standing on, and numerous climbs were opened with protection or 'aid' coming from mild steel pitons, or pegs, which can still be found littering many cracks in the European Alps. These were difficult to remove as they tended to deform into the rock if driven in enough to 'bite'. Resistance to aid climbing started to appear when climbers noticed that, on the popular climbs, the routes were becoming 'cluttered' with old, rusting, mild steel pitons, and that the constant insertion and removal of 'chrome-moly' pitons had

Yosemite is the forging ground of big-wall aid climbing. A (rare) bolt is being used to aid passage.

A typical bunch of big-wall aid gear. The small rounded 'nuts' are in fact malleable copperheads.

enlarged cracks, defacing the rock and leaving 'piton scars'. By this stage, many old aid routes had already been freed – mainly due to the high-friction rock boots and more user-friendly ropes and belay devices – and the advent of wired nuts and camming devices rendered pitons virtually obsolete. Aid climbing came to be considered as the domain of only a few dedicated 'lunatics', except for certain routes and areas that still needed aid to succumb. These tended to be on big walls, such as the Yosemite Valley, or other long routes with either technical difficulties that barred free climbing, or which were of such a nature that speed was essential and pulling on gear was considered acceptable.

AID CLIMBING EQUIPMENT

Modern aid climbing uses a wide range of equipment to enhance success. 'Clean' aid climbing (i.e. using gear which does not damage the rock when inserted or removed) is encouraged.

The standard gear discussed in the traditional rock climbing chapter is also used in aid climbing – chocks, camming devices, slings, and so on. The difference comes in quantity – a long aid pitch can require 40 to 50 chocks or camming devices, and 60 to 80 carabiners. Aid racks also include many small nuts, far smaller and more numerous than those on free-climbing racks. These are often required (and designed) only to take the climber's body weight, and not to hold a fall. They may be made of aluminium or brass (which deform into the rock and hold better), or steel (which is stronger, but can easily pull out).

Pitons come in a bewildering array of shapes and sizes, from the tiny RURP (Realized Ultimate Reality Piton), which is the size of a postage stamp and as thin as a knife blade, to huge bongs of 20cm (8in) in size.

Each piton style has specific uses – the popular lost arrow is good in a horizontal crack; angles are of use in larger cracks (although camming devices and nuts largely replace these); leepers work well stacked in bottoming cracks; bongs double as large chocks in wide or off-width cracks. The modern tendency is to use pitons only in cracks which are too small to take free-climbing gear. (*See* page 100.)

The real 'aid explosion' came in the 1960s following the creation of chrome-molybdenum pitons in America. These were far stronger than the mild steel being forged in Europe at the time; pitons could now be placed in thinner cracks, and were easily removed after use. As a result artificial climbing was forced into new realms of difficulty.

Piton hammer

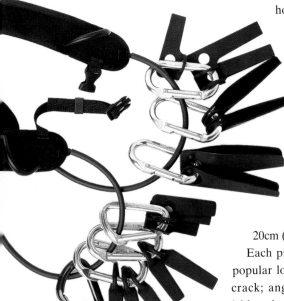
A selection of pitons on a bandolier (top to bottom): knifeblades, angles, leepers, and lost arrows.

In North America the exploration of the huge walls of Yosemite took place, while in Europe, sustained routes were opened on the large overhangs of the Dolomites. The 'Whack and Dangle' philosophy, as it was wryly called, spread to many areas of the climbing world, with aid routes (whole or partial) springing up in Europe, the UK, South America, South Africa, New Zealand and Australia.

Bashies are designed to hold a climber's weight (just!); their soft head melds into minute deformities on the rock. Copperheads consist of copper swaged onto a steel cable. Aluma heads are similar, but use slightly more malleable aluminium. Circleheads consist of two swages, and are used in horizontal cracks. Climbing on these demands complete commitment and places the routes in the upper aid grades (*see* page 152).

Bolts (discussed under sport climbing – *see* page 72) make a large difference to the quality of the route, albeit in the interests of safety. Most aid climbers give serious consideration to placing these and only do so when absolutely necessary, often only using them at main belay stances as the 'final back-up'. In Yosemite Valley, amongst other places, bolts now have to be placed by hand with no power drills allowed. This rule certainly makes the climber think twice before placing a bolt.

In addition to the above items and the normal complement of free climbing gear, one needs a selection of other specialized gear.

Étriers are ladder-like slings that allow one to step from one aid placement to the next. Two slightly differing schools have arisen although with a fair amount of preferential crossover.

In Europe, the current tendency is to use mini rope ladders with five or six aluminium bars as steps; in the American school, tied-off tape slings or sewn tape slings are used, often with doubled or strengthened bars to prevent the slings from closing. Most aid climbers make use of two or more étriers.

A useful tip when you are making knotted aid étriers is to buy tape equal to three times the length of the sling (a 1.5m; 5ft) étrier with five steps – i.e. five overhand knots – requires 4.5m, or 15ft, of tape). Étriers should be connected to the harness or a carabiner by a long piece of accessory cord in case they are dropped, and to assist in retrieval from above.

Daisy chains (slings with loops knotted or sewn every 10cm, or 4in, or so) allow for quick attachment from the harness to anchor points or étrier steps for resting. Once again, two daisy chains are often carried to allow for versatility.

Fifi hooks may be used at the end of étriers, daisy chains or simple slings. These open metal hooks allow for quick clipping and unclipping from aid pieces but unhook easily. Always back one up with a carabiner if it is being used as a main rest piece.

Double gear racks, with plenty of attachment slings, are used to carry the vast quantity of protection and carabiners. These allow weight to be distributed evenly, reducing neck strain. Many are sensibly designed to double as a chest harness, allowing for better rest on overhangs or when ascending with jumars.

Belay seats are fabric nappies (diapers) used for hanging belays. They are not, however, designed to be the sole point of attachment in hanging belays, so climbers should be careful – always clip main points to the harness as well.

Ascenders, such as jumars, are absolutely essential when you are hauling gear as well as for seconding pitches in major big-wall aid ascents.

Piton hammers have a flat side for hitting in the pitons, and a sharper pick for copperheads or for cleaning cracks. The hammer is attached to the harness with a sling which allows the climber full above-head extension; holsters on the harness or climbing pack are useful.

Bathooks or skyhooks are a great help for moving upwards, although a certain delicacy is required as it is only the tips of the hooks that lodge precariously in the rock. Often the tips are filed, and there is a wide variety of single and double tips.

Daisy chain

Pulleys for hauling gear bags are also required by big-wall climbers. Those with bearings, although costly, allow the rope to run more easily under load. Some pulleys even have auto-brakes, which are usually cam-type devices designed to prevent the haul sack from slipping back.

Haul bags are used to hold equipment. These have a smooth, strong top – allowing them to be pulled past obstructions – and are designed to be snag-free. A weak haul bag which collapses on a major route is disastrous; it is wise to make sure you choose a tried and tested brand.

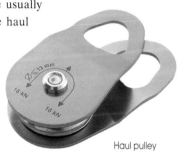

Haul pulley

Cheatsticks enable climbers to clip pieces of gear high above them. They hold the carabiner solidly open, only allowing it to spring free once it has been clipped in place.

Kneepads help to protect the knees when jumaring or climbing.

Gloves can help when hauling or jumaring, or in some crack systems.

Portaledges or **hammocks** make long nights spent out on the rock bearable, and newer versions, such as bat-tents, provide a roofed cover.

The usual supply of **bivouac gear** – sleeping bags, water containers, stove and cooking gear, food, rain gear, warm clothing – is also needed. Plenty of water is always a good idea as aid routes often take longer than anticipated and dehydration is a common problem. You need at least 5 litres (9 pints) per active day. On long aid routes in places like Yosemite Valley, aid climbers often haul a bewildering array of goods up the wall, including stereo sets, gas heaters, portaloos and other creature comforts, but this is the exception rather than the rule.

Sky hook

Étriers

99

To negotiate a tough aid section of a big wall route successfully requires careful piton placement.

Home from home – all of their belongings tied to a few points on the rock in the Yosemite Valley.

Worth taking note of is the 'take it in, take it out' philosophy prevalent in places such as Yosemite. Because of the pressure of numbers, even human waste must be carried out. Several ingenious methods are now employed, such as hollow plastic pipes and 'fold up' cardboard boxes with liners.

The once prevalent practice of 'tossing the gear off the top' after finishing the route has been stopped; not only is this practice hazardous to climbers and the public below, but gear often gets invisibly damaged on landing (not to mention the cost factor!). These days it has to be carried down.

PITON PLACEMENTS

Good   Good   Good if bashed in   Poor   Poor   Better

By using different-coloured ropes as well as climbing webbing used in daisy chains or étriers, confusion can be reduced.

AID PLACEMENTS

In general, the rule is 'place each piece as high above the previous one as practically possible'. This cuts down on time and gear. Rope drag should be minimized, as there are usually plenty of carabiners for the rope to pass through. The European method uses two 9mm ropes; the American method usually one 10mm or 11mm rope.

Placing aid climbing gear is not very different to that of traditional climbing (*see* previous chapter), except that each piece now **has** to take strain. In aid climbing you also normally clip the carabiner straight into the piece of gear, so as to maximize height gain.

Placing Pitons

Generally, horizontal placements are more secure, and piton eyes should point downwards. Select the pin to fit the crack – never try to force gear in.

A good piton rings with a high-pitched 'ping' with the final hammer strokes. Tap the piton after placement to test for rotation. Use slings right against the rock to tie off under- or overdriven pitons, so as to minimize torque. Pitons can often be stacked or nested in large cracks. Remember to tie off the stacked pitons with nonloadbearing 'keeper' slings in order to catch them in case the placement fails.

Placing Malleable Placements

When using copperheads and the like, the piece should be inserted into the crack or flare, then hit into place, or 'pasted', using an 'x' format – top right, bottom left, and so on. Once pasted in, it should be tested for movement. If it moves, repaste it.

Malleable heads should be used circumspectly – they often just manage to support the climber's body weight. Using them has been likened to walking on year-old rotten eggs which have been precracked!

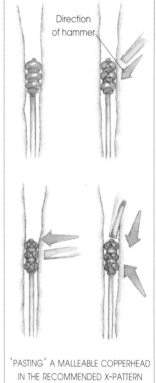

'PASTING' A MALLEABLE COPPERHEAD IN THE RECOMMENDED X-PATTERN

AID CLIMBING TECHNIQUES

Living vertically produces interesting problems, probably the most frequent and annoying being dropped gear. All items should have tie-in loops (duct tape can be used on items like water bottles, to both strengthen them and give a clip-in point).

Good   Unsafe   Weak

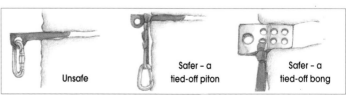

Unsafe   Safer – a tied-off piton   Safer – a tied-off bong

TOP-STEPPING

Here a daisy chain (blue) under tension is used to hold the climber in balance.

STARTING THE CLIMB

After attaching to the rope, racking all gear, and arranging your belay:

1. Look around and place an aid piece as high as is practically possible.

2. Attach the étrier and slowly stand up onto the piece. Give a small 'bounce' to test it or, if you are unsure of it, gently 'ooze' your body weight onto it.

3. Clip your daisy chain in and then clip your rope into a second carabiner on the piece of protection.

4. Climb up the étrier until the point of aid is at waist level, then re-clip the daisy chain or clip your second chain to the protection to give a rest position. (Beware of outward force being exerted on a protection intended to hold downwards force – it may suddenly give way.)

5. Reach up and place the next point, clip in your second étrier and proceed as before. Remember to retrieve your first étrier and clip it to your harness.

With solid placements, 'top stepping' can be done – this gives great height advantages although it is a bit unnerving. By clipping the daisy chain to the lower placement, a triangle of forces can be set up, giving greater stability (*see* illustration, top left).

Resting is essential: by using the feet as a rest or hooking in with fifi hooks, you can maximize rest opportunities. Clipping in the gear harness as a chest harness can relieve the strain on the back and neck during rests. In aid climbing, as in free climbing, do as much work with your legs as possible – arms tire far more easily than legs.

TENSION TRAVERSES AND PENDULUMS

These enable the climber to move over horizontal sections of rock. In a tension traverse, the second holds the leader on a tight rope, allowing him to

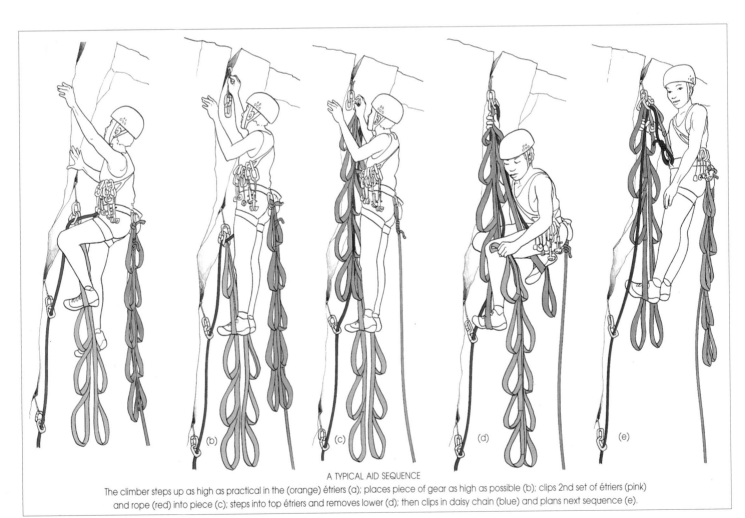

A TYPICAL AID SEQUENCE

The climber steps up as high as practical in the (orange) étriers (a); places piece of gear as high as possible (b); clips 2nd set of étriers (pink) and rope (red) into piece (c); steps into top étriers and removes lower (d); then clips in daisy chain (blue) and plans next sequence (e).

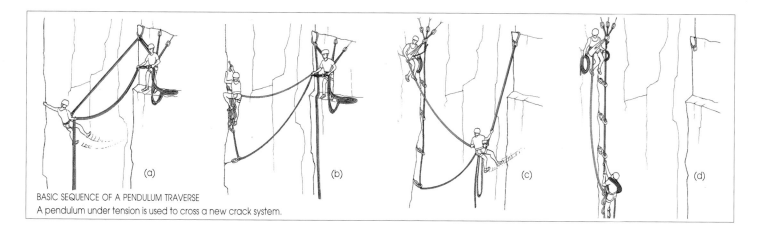

BASIC SEQUENCE OF A PENDULUM TRAVERSE
A pendulum under tension is used to cross a new crack system.

make use of the rope as a stabilizing point when standing on small holds or marginal points of aid on a more-or-less horizontal traverse.

Pendulums make the crossing of larger blank sections possible; for example, where you want to cross from a crack which blanks out to an adjacent, continuing crack system. In a situation like this, the leader places a 'bomber' anchor as high in the first crack as possible; he is then lowered off until there

is enough rope to allow him to run back and forth across the intervening wall until he has worked up sufficient momentum to enable him to reach the second crack.

The leader then places gear in this and moves up high enough to belay the second in the same movement. In pendulums, using two ropes can allow the second a far safer pendulum, as there is a safety back-up in case of one rope fraying.

Bottom left A climber relies on precarious aid points.

Below El Capitan is one of the Yosemite peaks associated with the climbing exploits of Royal Robbins.

ROYAL ROBBINS

The name of Royal Robbins is inextricably linked with the sheer granite walls of Yosemite Valley. Born in 1935, Royal was already an accomplished boulderer at 15, and the young prodigy soon set his sights on climbing in Yosemite. At 19 he climbed his first Yosemite route, the second ascent of Yosemite Point Buttress. Robbins then went on to make the second ascent of the Salathe-Steck route on the North Face of the Sentinel, still regarded as one of the best routes in the Valley.

In 1957, Royal rocketed to fame when he conquered the 610m (2000ft) vertical, previously unclimbed face of Half Dome's great North West Face. Robbins then returned to Yosemite, after two years of compulsory military service, to snatch the second ascent of the Nose of El Capitan route in a record time of

6½ days. His next route was the South West Face of El Capitan. This was considered 'unclimbable without hundreds of bolts'; together with two team members Royal spent nine days on the wall and climbed it with only 13 bolts. The route became known as the Salathe Wall and is regarded as one of the world's ultimate climbs.

HANGING BELAYS

On aid climbs, good belays are of vital significance. A hanging belay can generate immense confusion as both climbers eventually meet there before the start of the next pitch. Organization and teamwork are absolutely essential.

Place a good number of points, and connect them all to one another and primarily to the main belay anchor (especially yourself). Remember that these placements might take considerable strain if the leader falls, the haul sack gets jammed, or while the second jumars – or 'jugs' (as it is often called in this branch of the sport) – up the tied-off rope. Normal practice is for the leader to haul the sack while or before the second jugs, in case it gets stuck en route.

SECONDING AID ROUTES

This is an art in itself and can be more exhilarating than leading, particularly on overhanging ground or traverses, where spectacular swings may have to be taken after removing a piece of gear.

The second will usually jumar up a major route (although it is easier to simply aid through overhangs), cleaning the gear out along the way. He does not untie from the end of the rope but lets it 'follow' him, and usually ties repeatedly in to the rope using a figure 8 knot as he climbs. This is in case of jumar failure or problems in moving jumars past protection points. On reaching the belay, the second gathers and racks the protection gear, and usually leads on.

It is worth remembering that ropes wear rapidly over rock edges – avoid 'bouncing' when jumaring, and avoid swings where possible. When cleaning pitons, hammer gently back and forth until they come loose. Another method is to connect a daisy chain to the piton via a carabiner, enabling you to jerk the piton out (a piton hammer with a hole in it forms a useful 'hammer-swing' as the inertia of the hammer head helps to jerk the piton loose). Malleable pieces can seldom be successfully removed, and are often best left for the next climbers to use.

When jumaring on traverses or overhangs, the top jumar has to be moved past an aid piece before it can be removed. The lower jumar could be pulled

Left *Although cumbersome, a haul bag enables one to carry sufficient provisions when tackling a long climb.*

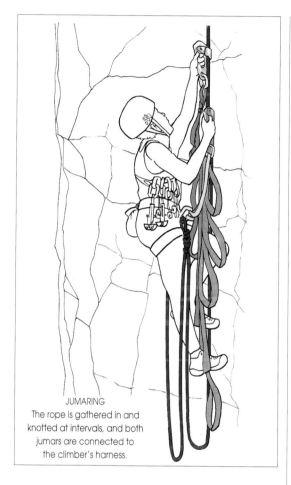

JUMARING
The rope is gathered in and
knotted at intervals, and both
jumars are connected to
the climber's harness.

into the piece and jam, so keep the lower jumar as
low as possible when moving the top jumar past the
piece, or use a French prusik to replace the lower
ascender as this can be slid down under load.

OVERHANGS

When leading overhangs, have ascenders or prusik
loops close to hand. If a protection piece pulls out,
you may have no other way back to the rock from
your hanging perch out in space.

On overhangs, the use of two daisy chains and at
least two étriers helps keep you closer to the rock
and able to resist the tendency to swing off balance.
Overhangs are nerve-racking, but are seldom more
difficult or dangerous than vertical aid climbing. Stay
relaxed to save energy and increase efficiency.

Right Many older aid routes are now free climbed
using modern tools and techniques.

Right and opposite right
Dwarfed by soaring rock,
climbers take up the challenge
to reach the summit.

Opposite left A long runout
on a granite wall in Namibia.

SACK-HAULING

The haul sack often becomes the most cursed item on a big wall, seemingly getting heavier as the days wear on. Hauling it requires effort, but energy can once again be saved by efficient principles:

1. Keep the locking jumar or auto-brake short, to avoid up-and-down movement every time you restart the haul sequence.

2. Use either your legs or your body weight to do the haul via a jumar or ascender of some sort.

3. 'Wall walking' if the sack is very heavy also helps. Allow yourself 2 to 3m (6.5 to 10ft) of slack, then walk down the wall, pulling the sack. Climb back up the étrier, move the hauling jumar up, and repeat.

4. A thin back-rope to the second can help to free the sack if it jams. It also helps to direct the sack under overhangs.

EMERGENCY RETREATS

As much as bolts are considered an anathema, carrying a small hand-bolting kit may make retreat possible in a storm or emergency. Always have a back-up plan for worst-case scenarios.

CHAPTER SEVEN

SNOW AND ICE CLIMBING
The Lure of Winter

The joys of ice climbing!

Snow and ice climbing can range from mild walks on snow-covered peaks or easy glaciated terrain to all of the drama of 8000m (26,250ft) expeditions. In essence, much of the equipment and a lot of the technique is applicable to all forms, although the more extreme the experience, the more specialized the equipment and skills required.

'Good' snow and ice climbs are rarely a leisurely pursuit. Often the days are short and the cold makes spending too much time on the route both unpleasant and dangerous. Swift, efficient movement, inventiveness in finding and placing protection gear, and often considerable boldness are required. Nonetheless, it can be a pleasurable and satisfying experience, and competence in snow and ice work is essential if you are to do any worthwhile alpine routes or big mountains.

Snow and ice climbing is a complex and intricate subject, which takes a good deal of time and practice to master. In this chapter, the equipment will be discussed first in order to introduce the prospective ice climber to the range of options. This will be followed by an outline of the techniques used.

CLOTHING

Once again, much of the basic equipment is that of the traditional rock climber – ropes, belay devices, slings, carabiners, and protection gear.

However, the personal 'warm-and-wet' gear is radically different to that required for the average 'day at the crag'.

Modern ice boots

Climber on Marble Falls, Colorado, USA. This fragile water ice needs delicate ice axe technique.

BOOTS

Snow and ice boots need to be rigid enough to take crampons, while also being comfortable enough for extended walking. In general, the boot should have a high ankle in order to provide adequate support, and should be both warm and waterproof. Most climbers would agree that the 'perfect' boot has yet to be designed – and thus your choice usually comes down to a compromise determined by the type of snow and ice climbing to be undertaken, and personal preferences. Boots made from both leather and from plastic are available.

109

Leather boots are the traditional option and have been in use since time immemorial. They have many drawbacks – they are not very waterproof and can become waterlogged and heavy. They require careful and constant drying and waterproofing, and can be stiff and uncomfortable when new or cold. However, for one-day routes, mixed climbs (rock and ice) or easy ice routes, their lightness and comfort are a bonus and they are more than adequate, providing the correct choice of crampon has been made.

Plastic boots (or 'plastics') are the new wave and are becoming increasingly popular, despite their usually steep price tag. With a double layer consisting of a plastic shell and a lined inner boot, plastics provide considerable warmth and yet still manage to be relatively light. The shell can be made of a number of hi-tech materials, including various polycarbonates and carbon fibre. Makes of plastic boots can be found which offer extreme degrees of insulation for winter climbing or expedition work, although these can become rather large and cumbersome.

Plastics are totally waterproof, although this in itself can become a nuisance as condensation inside the boot may cause wet and cold feet from the inside out. Nonetheless, there is no doubt that under severe conditions your feet stay warmer and drier than in leather boots.

Plastics can be totally rigid, enabling 'step-in' crampons to be fitted; this is a great advantage when battling with cold, clumsy hands. When fitting plastic boots, the fit of the inner boot is more critical than that of the outer. Wearing socks, put on the inner without the shell. There should be about 2cm (¾ in) space at your heel. Now you need to find a shell that properly fits the comfortable inner. Don't be afraid to downsize or upsize shells as some manufacturers use the same liner for a number

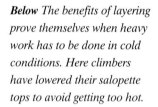

Below The benefits of layering prove themselves when heavy work has to be done in cold conditions. Here climbers have lowered their salopette tops to avoid getting too hot.

of different shell sizes. Be prepared to spend both time and money to get the right pair – your comfort and perhaps your life may depend on it.

GAITERS

These are essential to prevent snow from falling into the top of the boot, as well as to aid insulation. For short routes with minimal walk-in (approach) over snow, short ankle gaiters will suffice; for more elaborate needs, full-length gaiters are required. Some overgaiters cover the whole boot, from toe to heel, with a rubber 'boot' that clamps down onto the rand of the boot, totally preventing laces from icing over. Overgaiters are difficult to put on and remove, and are generally simply left in place on the boot. Try these on before buying, and check that they open fully enough to allow you to remove the inner boot easily if necessary. They must also allow access to the lacing system. Overgaiters can be lined to provide extra insulation for long, serious climbs.

SOCKS

Warm, thick socks are the norm; many climbers swear by the use of one thinner inner pair and a thick outer pair in order to reduce blisters. Beware of too many pairs, as boots that are too tight actually end up making your feet colder by reducing circulation. Socks made of fleece or wetsuit material are now on offer, and these have their adherents who will sing their praises. Once again, it is advisable to do some experimentation to find the best combination for your purposes.

GLOVES

These are essential for snow and ice climbing. Many climbers choose a very thin inner pair made of silk, polypropylene or similar material, with a 'working' pair over these. For serious ice climbing, the outer gloves should have palms with leather or roughened nylon or rubber to aid grip on the axes; they must also be padded, both for warmth and to prevent knuckle crushing from using ice axes. Shrunken wool mitts are still popular, although they are not waterproof and their thickness prevents you from handling equipment easily. Fibre-pile, especially newer 'windbloc' fleeces, works well. Outer gloves of Goretex or a similar material are useful in bad weather or if the snow gets wet. A number of new 'super-mitt' double-glove models have a Goretex outer with a built-in fleece or fibre-pile inner glove.

Outer gloves should be connected to the wrist or elsewhere via an elastic or lanyard, as it is all too easy to drop gloves when removing them to allow for finer, more delicate work. Dropped gloves can be a tragedy, and it is advisable to carry a spare pair in each party.

BALACLAVA

An amazing amount of body heat can be lost through the head so a cap and/or balaclava is essential. If wearing a helmet, then a thinner silk or fleece balaclava will suffice, but take a warmer one for bivouacs or long walk-ins to huts or crags.

BODY LAYERS

The concept of 'layering' – using a number of lighter weight garments of differing properties in place of one or two heavier items – has undoubtedly found favour with climbers.

By combining various materials and styles, you can open or close layers as temperature or humidity changes; by using a number of layers, air, a prime insulating material, is trapped between them.

For the first layer, choose soft and comfortable **thermal underwear** made of hi-tech fibres that 'wick' away moisture from the skin. Over this goes a **shirt layer**, made of low-absorption polypropylene fabric, thin fleece (the term refers to man-made fluffy fibre-pile material, usually polyester) or wool; then a thicker fleece or similar synthetic-layer **pullover** or **jacket**. A vast array of these faces the buyer, and you must choose according to taste and practicality. Smoother fleeces are sometimes not as warm but, if used without a shell layer, they are less prone to collecting windblown snow which might

later melt. Denser fleeces are more windproof and even partially showerproof. Shop around, take the manufacturers' claims with a healthy pinch of salt and find garments that are comfortable, don't have too many gadgets and are easy to use. Fleeces have high insulation properties, but unless they are made of 'windbloc' or something similar, are not windproof. Again, two thin layers are better than one thick one, allowing for greater variety in temperature regulation.

On the legs, **long-john thermal underwear** is worn, with **breeches** or **salopettes** on top. Salopettes, which consist of leggings with a 'bib' in front and a flap at the back, and are held up by suspenders (braces), are excellent in preventing snow and ice from drifting in around the midriff. For serious climbing, you should be able to zip salopettes completely on or off via side zips without having to remove your boots. Some sort of 'flap' for toilet stops is very useful, even though inelegant!

The **outer layer** must combine windproof and waterproof properties. The modern, 'breathable' materials form efficient if costly shell layers. Despite the controversies that rage about the subject, there is little doubt that Goretex (or similar materials) really works. These materials allow the moisture generated by the climber during exertion to escape from the body to a certain extent, while also preventing the climber from getting too wet.

Left A climber wearing full multi-layered alpine kit.

Retractable
ski poles

Remember to try on shell systems with all the likely base layers you will wear – shells that are too small or too large can become very frustrating. Ensure that the sleeves are long enough when working above your head, and that leggings allow for high steps.

The **jacket** needs some specific features: it should have a good hood, with a drawstring to close the face in rain or snow. The hood must be capable of accommodating a helmet underneath – some excellent designs allow for an extension to be unclipped for this purpose. A piece of flexible wire in the front rim helps to keep the hood off the eyes, and deflect rain and snow. The front zip (and in fact, all zips) should be sturdy and capable of being easily zipped open and closed. Watch out for 'finicky' zipper systems that are difficult to connect. A flap should cover the zip to keep spindrift (windblown snow) out. It should be possible to adjust the size of cuffs, and seal them off to prevent the entry of snow or ice from axes wielded above the head. Articulated sleeves (ones that have extra foldaway joints under the armpit) are excellent for axe-wielding, as they reduce the tightness which otherwise restricts arm action and can tire you out. A word of warning on Velcro – some types do not work well in freezing conditions or when iced up. Check that a suitable type has been used. Good, old-fashioned pop-studs are a viable option.

Easily accessible pockets with closure flaps are useful for everything from that vital piece of chocolate to compasses or your route descriptions.

Often the outer layer garments have reinforced patches on key areas, such as the knees, seat, and elbows. An emerging notion is to make climbing gear very 'trendy', and increasing numbers of people who might never see a hill in their life are proudly sporting climbing brand names. Much of the truly functionally designed climbing gear will, however, simply not look good in the local nightclub, although conversely, it might just increase your status in the climbing bars of Chamonix!

Walking axe

TECHNICAL GEAR
RUCKSACK
For one-day routes, a sack with a volume of 40 to 50 litres (70 to 90 pints) is required. A simple style without too many pockets or straps is best, as it prevents snagging. Light weight is an advantage, as is a stabilizing padded hip belt. A body-contouring form makes it easier to use.

HARNESS
The harness needs to have both adjustable waist and leg loops to allow for clothing changes. Chest or full-body harnesses are popular with many alpinists who anticipate traversing crevassed areas. A full-body harness prevents the climber turning upside down if he falls into a crevasse; with a standard waist harness the weight of the pack often causes the climber to 'flip' when falling, making self-rescue much more difficult.

ICE AXE
This is the universal 'multitool' of snow and ice climbing. There are two primary forms: walking (long) axes and technical (short) axes.

Walking axes act as walking sticks, aiding balance and giving security on easy-angled snow and ice, and are used to arrest falls, or as a belay point.

Avoid taking too long an axe, as on slopes this will force your uphill axe-holding hand too high. If the axe is to be used for long, easily angled glacier walks, then get one where your hand just rests on the head when standing on level ground (70 to 75cm, or 27 to 30in is about right for the average adult).

The basic design of walking axes has not altered for centuries except for the hi-tech materials now used in their construction. They have a one-piece head with a gently curved pick, a large adze, and a long straight shaft. Wooden shafts lack strength if used for axe belays.

Walking axes generally have a short leash attached to the neck, which can slide down the shaft to allow for step cutting or for using the axe as an ice tool, and a thinner long leash attached to the harness to prevent the axe being lost if dropped whilst changing hands or when resting on slopes. Make this leash long enough so that you can use the axe in either hand on quite steeply angled slopes.

Alpine pack

112

As the angle attacked gets steeper and the ice harder, so you move into the realm of **technical axes** or 'ice tools'. Here the axe is not only used for balance, but as a tool to hook into the ice in order to provide the climber with leverage. It is also used as a hammer or 'screwdriver' for placing or removing gear, or as a belaying point. Technical axes tend to be from 45 to 60cm (17 to 24in) in length, and have short, generally curved shafts, modular heads and gruesome-looking picks.

In a modern technical axe look for:

• A head which is well balanced – heavy enough to get some force, but not too heavy. The steeper and harder the ice, the heavier the head needs to be – and the more tired you are going to get. Some models allow for weights to be added or removed.

• A hole big enough to take a carabiner for belaying as well as the wrist loop attachment.

The head will have a pick, and an adze or hammer. Modular design on modern ice tools allows for these to be changed to suit the occasion. Generally only the pick is ever changed, so a fully modular axe is an unnecessary luxury. Hammer heads are useful on a technical axe if you anticipate using it to drive in ice screws or pitons.

The **pick** has evolved the most over the years. A pick that has a 65- to 70-degree angle from the shaft is fine for most general mountaineering, but for steep, hard ice a reverse-curve pick of 50 to 60 degrees is favoured. The pick will have teeth of some kind to grip the ice – get fairly aggressive teeth if you are going for the serious stuff. Modern steel composites allow for thin but effective picks; tube-like picks are available for certain slushy water ice as opposed to hard crystalline ice.

The angle of the end is called the clearance. This affects the axe's ability to brake on self-arrest (the process, discussed later, whereby a falling climber rescues himself from a slide). A neutral or negative clearance pick drags on hard steep ice, hindering self-arrest; too positive a pick may hook in too rapidly, causing it to be torn from the climber's hand. However, it is difficult to self-arrest on seriously steep slopes, thus, to some extent, pick angles have become somewhat academic.

Technical
ice axe

The **adze** is used for cutting steps (a less common practice these days) or clearing snow from harder ice before placing an ice screw.

In today's extreme ice climbing, the axe is often used to 'torque' into rock cracks or between the ice and rock, and picks, adzes and hammers are often designed specifically with this in mind. Technical climbers usually use one axe with an adze, and one with a hammer.

The **shaft** of an ice axe is nowadays made from kevlar-based composites or advanced metal alloys, unlike the older wooden shafts. In a technical axe, if you value your knuckles, look for a curved shaft which will keep your hand away from the ice when you are striking. Test the swing, and choose an axe that complements your technique. The grip on the shaft is important, as having to grip unnecessarily hard to prevent sliding can tire you. A hard rubber covering is best, both to dampen shock and to improve your grip.

An often neglected factor is the **wrist loop** or ice axe leash. This takes the strain off the hand when climbing steep ice, and allows the climber to drop the axe when placing protections or using rock holds. Most leashes supplied with axes are rather poor quality so it is worth spending a bit extra to get a good one. An easily adjustable wrist loop with an adjustable length makes it easier to use the axe in different conditions. You should be able to tighten and loosen the loop with your teeth when it's on your arm. Having the length exactly right allows for better rests and greater efficiency. Usually the loop should sit roughly level with the spike on the bottom end of the axe. Choose one that is strong enough to act as a belay sling – this will save time and trouble at stances.

For periods of rock or mixed climbing, or when belaying, short axes are often placed in holsters on the harness or on the hip belt of the pack. Hammer holsters are a worthwhile investment.

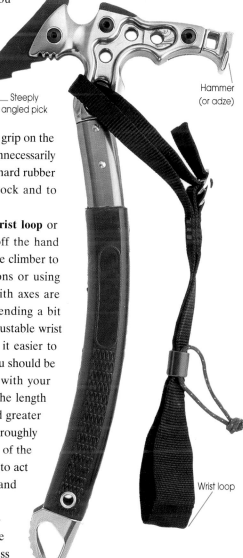

Steeply angled pick

Hammer (or adze)

Wrist loop

Spike   PREDATOR ICE AXE

*Strap-on crampons are better
suited to flexible leather boots.*

CRAMPONS

The shepherds of Europe first used primitive crampons, consisting of spikes tied to their boot heels to assist them in moving on the slippery snow. The first 'modern' crampons were produced in the early 1900s by England's Oscar Eckenstein; he created eight-point crampons which tied onto the whole rigid boot he also pioneered. Initially crampons had eight or 10 points but no 'front points', thus movement uphill was achieved by cutting steps with the axe – a long and tiring process. In the late 1930s 12-point crampons were developed, although they only really came into use in the 1950s (exactly who first introduced these is a difficult question, as at least five climbers of differing nationality all claim precedence). These revolutionized ice climbing as the two extra front points allowed climbers to move up very steep faces without needing to cut steps.

General-purpose crampons are hinged 12-point crampons. The hinge allows the crampon to be fitted to boots that are not fully rigid, and a series of crisscross straps prevents the crampon from slipping off. Although these crampons are fine for normal glacier and snow travel, they are not ideal for steep technical ice. They tend to have wide, horizontal, fixed front points.

The **technical ice-climbing crampon** is usually also a 12-pointer, although some now have a 13th point as a 'spike' or 'monopoint' in the very front middle. The technical crampon is rigid or semi-rigid, and requires plastic boots. Variations on claw length and angle as well as type of fitting and metal can be found, and the final choice is rather complex and personal. Suffice it to say that climbers seem to favour moderately curved points for steep ice. Modular front points are available, allowing for different choices for differing conditions. Vertical front points have replaced horizontal ones for steep ice.

Rigid crampons are expensive, heavier than flexible ones, and clumsy to walk on. They are, however, better suited to steep ice as they support the foot and allow for more precise placement. Semi-rigid crampons are the most popular choice with alpinists and occasional climbers.

Crampons should fit properly. Spend some time ensuring that this is the case – there is simply nothing worse than a crampon detaching halfway up a desperate ice climb! Many climbers still favour

strap-on crampons, although with plastic boots clip-in bindings make life much easier and are surprisingly secure despite their apparent simplicity. The bindings fit onto the boots (plastic boots are made with this in mind) via a baling-wire clip at the toe and a snap-on clip lever at the heel. An adjustable leash around the ankle helps to keep the heel-clip tight, and prevents the climber losing the crampon if the clip comes loose. It is wise to carry adjustment tools and a spare nylon crampon strap in your pack, particularly if the crampons are untried in the field. Neoprene-coated nylon straps are excellent as they have virtually no stretch – a common fault with many ordinary nylon bindings.

Another useful tip is either to buy or make 'anti-balling plates'. These are simply smooth plastic or rubber coverings on the bottom of the crampon which reduce the balling up of snow as you walk. Similarly, it is worth investing in crampon protectors that cover the points when carrying the crampons in or on your sack.

Crampon points should be periodically sharpened, using a hand file rather than an electrical grinder which might detemper the metal. You file downwards on the front points and the edges of side spikes. It is not necessary to make the points too sharp as they would then wear down too fast.

ICE PROTECTION

Ice protection gear ('ice pro') varies, it has been said, from the sublime to the ridiculous. As standards advance, so ice pro becomes more and more marginal. However, for the novice ice climber on well-chosen routes, it can be both solid and reliable.

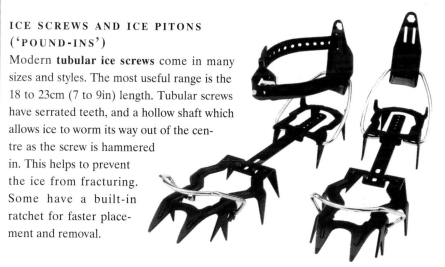

Modern step-in semi-rigid crampons.

ICE SCREWS AND ICE PITONS ('POUND-INS')

Modern **tubular ice screws** come in many sizes and styles. The most useful range is the 18 to 23cm (7 to 9in) length. Tubular screws have serrated teeth, and a hollow shaft which allows ice to worm its way out of the centre as the screw is hammered in. This helps to prevent the ice from fracturing. Some have a built-in ratchet for faster placement and removal.

Solid ice screws offer good protection in below-freezing temperatures, but are no good in wet or 'crumbly' ice. They suffer from melt-out (they loosen in the ice) because of limited thread displacement, and tend to break the ice on insertion or when under load. They are also difficult to remove. Their advantage lies in the ease and speed of placement.

A good compromise is the hammer-in screw-out type, such as the **scrube**. These have small threads and a hollow tube and work well in hard cold ice, but not in temperatures above freezing. It is usually best to buy the medium-length screws and pitons, as these can always be tied off close to the ice if you cannot drive them in all the way. Long screws might be needed in rotten or alpine ice, or 'aerated' water ice (which is more or less 'compacted snow'). A fatter tube spreads the load and supports more weight but is heavier.

Ice screws can be certified according to CE and UIAA standards, but many climbers regard the current tests to be unrealistic. A UIAA stamp would certainly guarantee a modicum of design approval, but a lack of one does not imply an inferior product. If you buy a reputable make, you will be as safe as you can get. A word of warning: in climbing circles, a current joke is the 'Russian ice screw'. Many thousands of titanium ice screws have been produced in Russia (presumably in ex-military factories). Some are excellent, in league with the best of the West, but others fail at alarmingly low loads. Once again, look for a reputable dealer and a reputable make.

Ice hooks provide protection in ice cracks, thin ice, and ice-filled rock cracks. This protection is usually pretty marginal, but the addition of an ice hook or two to the rack could make the difference between success or failure.

Warthog – a type of solid ice screw.

SNOW PROTECTION

Only two forms of manufactured snow protection are usually recognized – the deadman and snow stakes. They spread the load over a wide area of good, compact snow.

Deadman: a spade-shaped alloy plate, 20 by 25cm (8 by 10in), with a long wire attached to its centre. Correct placement is vital (*see* page 122).

Deadman

Snow stakes: seldom used because of the inconvenience of carrying them, they can be most useful in the loose snow and fluted columns of the Andes of South America or in the Himalayas, for example. Usually made of V- or T-shaped angled aluminium alloy, snow stakes are 50 to 75cm (20 to 30in) long, and have an arm width of between 5 and 10cm (2 to 4in). Holes are often drilled in order to lighten the stake. Like a deadman,

A sample of ice and rock gear, including a number of varied ice screws.

snow stakes have a long cable attached just above the midpoint. Most snow stakes allow for varied fastening heights.

Other protection used in snow involves ice axes or snow bollards (*see* page 123).

MISCELLANEOUS EQUIPMENT

SNOW GOGGLES AND SUNGLASSES

Snow reflects ultraviolet (UV) light, which can cause extensive damage to the cornea and retina of the eye. The higher the altitude, the less the UV light has been attenuated by the atmosphere, thus the greater the risk of snow blindness.

A good pair of glacier glasses (dark sunglasses) can not only help to reduce the UV danger, but can also protect the eyes from flying chips of ice when climbing. Side shields help to reduce both glare from the sides as well as the entry of particles.

Goggles may be used in place of sunglasses and can be useful in strong wind, or when spindrift or ice chips are in the air. Ensure that they have adequate ventilation holes to prevent fogging.

SELF-RESCUE EQUIPMENT

It is usual on glaciated terrain to carry at least two prusik slings and one long sling, in case self-rescue becomes necessary (*see* page 122 for techniques).

Right Good snow – such as this in Langtang Himal, Nepal – can be exhilarating, but negotiating cornices always requires care.

SNOW TECHNIQUES

The texture of snow can vary from virtual powder to being almost as hard as true ice. The techniques used must thus be varied according to snow type, slope angle and aspect, and other more subtle circumstances such as the experience of the party.

In essence, 'snow' refers to a surface in which steps can be kicked and where you can – albeit with difficulty – make do without crampons. On ice, crampons are essential.

Soft snow presents no technical difficulties but requires much hard work. In soft snow, which can be waist to chest deep, the lead should be rotated frequently. Using telescopic ski-mountaineering sticks can save energy and aid balance, and many climbers now use these on all moderate terrain in preference to ice axes. These reduce jolting on knees and spine, and aid climbers on slippery ground, downhills and boulder hopping.

If a lot of soft deep snow is anticipated, then snowshoes or ski-mountaineering equipment is a good idea. Generally, however, a good stiff pair of boots and an ice axe are the basic tools.

Right An easy alpine ridge is traversed using ski poles for balance.

Far right Swift, efficient movement is required on snow and ice, as pictured here in Alpamayo, Peru.

KICKING STEPS

It is usual to kick steps while leaning on the axe for balance. You can ascend directly up a slope, but moving in diagonal lines often saves energy. To produce a secure step you may have to kick in a number of times, particularly in harder snow.

Steeper snow can be negotiated by varying the angle of the axe, and by using the pick or adze instead of the shaft. In diagonal lines, the axe is held uphill and can be used to 'lean' slightly into the slope. Avoid leaning too much, as this reduces the 'bite' of the boot. In very hard steep snow, you may have to ascend traverses by facing into the hill and kicking directly into the slope, although this is time-consuming and best avoided.

When descending, which is generally more difficult, you dig the heel into the snow by 'dropping' stiff-legged onto it facing outwards. On steep slopes, you may have to descend by facing into the slope and kicking steps directly down.

CUTTING STEPS

Nowadays, although largely superseded by the use of crampons, this can still be a useful technique if one of the party is tired or uncertain, or if crampons break or get lost. Climbers should note that it may also be quicker to cut a few steps up a steep short slope than to put on crampons. You must remember that the vast majority of major Alpine faces were originally climbed using step-cutting techniques – doing this as an exercise certainly creates a healthy respect for the pioneers!

The pattern of steps varies according to slope and snow type, but essentially follows the foot pattern you would use normally. Often a single line of steps enables good upward progress to be made; on really steep slopes a double line might be necessary.

Steps can be cut sideways (a technique known as 'slash' steps) with a single axe blow to allow diagonal upward movement – these are rapid and easy, but neither as secure nor as suitable in steep snow conditions as deeper 'bucket' steps. The latter require a few blows but serve for both hand- and footholds on steep snow.

Cutting steps on the downhill is far more difficult and it is often best to lower the lead climber, who can cut steps more easily and safely on belay. The second climber can then descend via these steps.

CUTTING STEPS ON A DIAGONAL

SELF-ARREST

If you slip on steepish snow, you can arrest your fall by judicious use of the ice axe. This technique needs practice, which should be done on a concave slope with a safe end-run.

The normal method is to force the pick of the axe into the hard snow as soon as is practical to avoid speed build-up. Beware of crampons digging into the slope – this may flip the climber or cause injury. Try to master the technique without crampons.

In order to self-arrest from a feet-first slide, grasp the axe head firmly with one hand and the bottom of the shaft with the other; then roll slowly onto the axe. The technique is most effective if the adze is held in the hand pressed into the collar bone, and the pick edged into the slope from about shoulder-height (*see* illustration opposite).

When sliding on your stomach, keep your feet up if wearing crampons to prevent them suddenly digging into the slope. If no crampons are worn, then the feet can be used to help brake.

In a head-first slide, try to use leverage on the dug-in pick to rotate your body into a foot-first slide.

The only true way to learn these techniques is to practise – this may well pay vast dividends later on. There are countless stories of climbers who have saved themselves from certain death through efficient (and sometimes lucky) braking action.

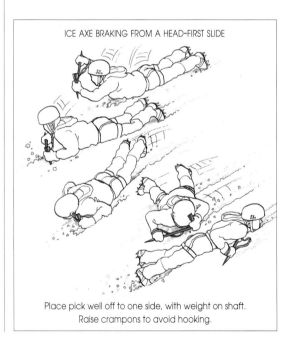

ICE AXE BRAKING FROM A HEAD-FIRST SLIDE

Place pick well off to one side, with weight on shaft.
Raise crampons to avoid hooking.

SELF-ARREST FROM A FEET-FIRST SLIDE

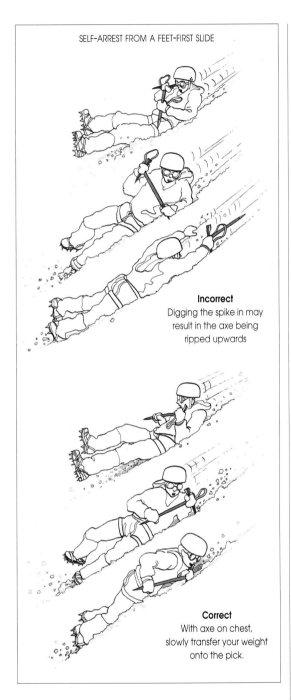

Incorrect
Digging the spike in may
result in the axe being
ripped upwards

Correct
With axe on chest,
slowly transfer your weight
onto the pick.

GLISSADING

Descending by means of a 'controlled slide' can be exhilarating as well as time- and energy-efficient. Learning to glissade goes hand-in-hand with snow-braking practice. You can glissade either standing, which is comfortable and elegant but demanding on the thigh muscles; crouching; or sitting, which demands a strong trouser seat!

GLACIER WALKING

The usual way to start serious snow and ice work is via glacier travel. Here the angles are not very steep and the snow is usually good. The danger here lies in the nature of glaciers – they move, and in moving, open up crevasses that may lie hidden under snow.

It is worth remembering that the most serious crevasses usually occur where the glacier steepens or bends suddenly. Glaciers tend to be at their most stable in the cold of early morning. 'Wet' glaciers (those covered with snow) are more dangerous than 'dry' glaciers, where crevasses are generally visible and can be avoided. Even so, unless the glacier is well known and demonstrably 'safe', it is advisable to rope up.

ROPING UP

The most serious glacier accidents happen to unroped parties. The use of a rope is an excellent safety measure, and can save time by allowing for more direct routes over 'suspicious' areas.

Shortening the rope around the body serves to make the rope more manageable, as a partial chest harness, and to allow rope for use in an emergency or give a belay over a particularly tricky section. Note that, after the coils are tied off with an over-hand knot, the rope is tied via a carabiner through the loop of this knot to the harness for safety. About 8 to 10m (26 to 33ft) of rope should be left between climbers as a minimum. Each climber now attaches a French prusik to the rope in front of him to allow for rescue, self-rescue or belay as the need arises.

THE CORRECT WAY TO SHORTEN THE ROPE

Left Glissading.

UNASSISTED HOIST
The climber is held
by his companions
(a); then the rope is
anchored on a prusik
(b); and the uninjured
climber prusiks out (c).
His pack is left hanging on
the rope to make lifting
the prusik loops easier,
and to reduce his weight.

ASSISTED HOIST
Note pulley, and ice axe on
crevasse lip, to reduce friction.

*Right A climber being
assisted out of a crevasse.*

CREVASSE RESCUE

If he is correctly roped up, a climber falling into a crevasse should be held by his companion(s). This is more likely if the person holding the fall is alert and the rope connecting the climbers is kept taut.

As the leader falls into the crevasse, a taut rope starts to cut into the edge, slowing the fall. By falling and sitting back with their heels dug in, the other climbers can hold the leader.

Often the victim can then climb out unaided. In this case, those holding the rope should move backwards as he climbs up, to ensure that the rope remains taut. Avoid rigging up a complicated rescue until it has been established that the victim cannot rescue himself.

The next alternative is for the fallen climber to prusik back up the rope – hence the value of a pre-placed prusik loop. Each climber should have at least two prusiks and a long sling. If the pack proves to be a problem, tie it off to the rope below the foot prusik to be hauled up later.

Should the fallen climber be unable to climb the rope, he may need to be hoisted. This is never easy, but has certainly saved many a life. The climber holding the fall must endeavour to place protection in the glacier (ice screws, deadmen or similar) and ease the load off onto this via a prusik loop. Obviously having three on the rope helps in this, as one can take the strain while the other prepares the belay. The rescue is effected using the pulley techniques discussed in Chapter Five.

SNOW BELAYS

These are seldom as secure as you would want them to be, but at times might be the only option. The consistency of snow can vary over very short distances so, to ensure the best possible anchor strength, it is often worth moving around a few metres from side to side and checking the snow.

In snow belays, the body position of the belayer is often the critical factor. It is best to sit spread-eagled in the snow in a 'trench' dug for the legs and seat. Body belays are a frequently used technique in these conditions, as any fall would be a slide rather than an abrupt fall. The body of the belayer can thus absorb some of the shock.

Often snow belays are used to allow climbers to descend steep slopes. The first climber is safeguarded from above, then the most able climber descends 'belayed' from below. For self-rescue of injured or exhausted climbers (when no external rescue team is available or required), it is important to be familiar with snow belays.

SNOW ANCHORS

The **deadman** needs to be placed at a critical angle of 40 degrees to the slope. This angle is estimated using the axe and back of the deadman. A 'step' is cut, and the deadman hammered in at the back of this at the correct angle. The wire should be kept taut and pulled through the snow. Ensure that the wire is tight to the centre of the plate and does not move up at an angle, or else it might tend to pull the deadman up and out.

The deadman functions best in hard snow, thus layers of soft snow might first have to be cleared from the surface. Take a stance a few metres below the deadman, and clip in only after pulling it hard to bed it into the snow.

Snow stakes are placed according to the angle of the slope. They tend to be used in insecure or unconsolidated snow. On less-steep slopes they are placed a few degrees back from the vertical, as the slope steepens, so they can go to 45 degrees to the slope.

Snow stakes can be hard to remove, and are often left *in situ*, especially after descents. They tend to be used in semi-melted snow and ice, such as that found in the Peruvian Andes or Nepalese Himalayas.

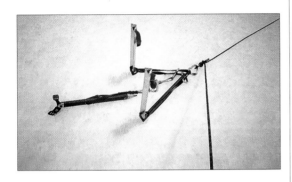

Snow bollards, cut some 20cm (8in) deep in a horseshoe shape with the broad top upwards, can be a useful anchor, effective in hard snow, and often used in descent. No kit has to be left and, with care, the rope can be retrieved. Take note though that under load, the rope can cut into the bollard and 'freeze' in place. It often helps to 'pad' the back of the slot with some material; axes, hammers, pegs, etc. can also be used if pushed vertically into the snow at the top of the bollard.

Axe anchors can take various forms and are very effective in well-consolidated snow. However, if incorrectly loaded, axes tend to rotate out. Various combinations are illustrated – the exact one used depends on snow conditions and the axes available.

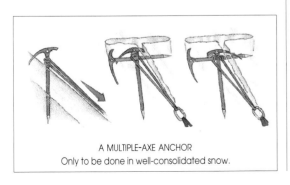

A MULTIPLE-AXE ANCHOR
Only to be done in well-consolidated snow.

The belay should be loaded from well below the axes to improve the angle of the sling.

With 'axe-and-foot combinations', the axe is pushed into the snow or ice above the foot, and braced against the boot. The rope is then led around the axe handle and the boot, giving a moderately substantial belay. This is used for security when lowering someone down a slightly angled slope.

TIPS AND TECHNIQUES OF GLACIER TRAVEL

• Keep the rope taut at all times.
• Walk at right angles to crevasses where possible.
• In badly crevassed areas, the leader should probe the ground ahead to confirm the security of snow bridges.
• When jumping crevasses, set up a temporary belay. If you do this, ensure there is sufficient slack in the rope.
• Fall forwards after jumping crevasses and drive the axe into the snow – the edges may not be solid.
• Watch for hollows in the snow which might indicate the presence of sub-surface crevasses.
• Figure 8 knots tied at 2m (6.5ft) intervals in the rope between climbers can help to arrest a fall into a crevasse. This can be especially useful with a 'rope' of two climbers, and also where the second climber is lighter than the first climber.

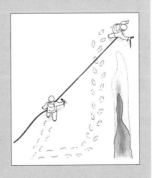

Left Multiple axes can be used as anchors in icy snow.

Far left The length of slings should be carefully adjusted so as to equalize tension on the anchors.

SITTING BODY BELAY
The climber makes full use of feet and hips to reduce strain on the single belay point.

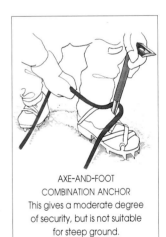

AXE-AND-FOOT COMBINATION ANCHOR
This gives a moderate degree of security, but is not suitable for steep ground.

Left inset The correct way to cross crevassed territory, with the leader at right angles to the suspected crevasse, the rope taut, and the second off to one side.

USING AMERICAN FOOT TECHNIQUE ON DESCENT

This helps to maintain stability and also allows for rapid descents.

ICE CLIMBING
USING CRAMPONS

Modern crampons are used in two ways: flatfooting, or French technique, and front pointing, or direct technique. These are used in different conditions, with climbers using a combination of the two styles. Cramponing demands trust in the equipment, balance, and confidence.

French technique may appear awkward at first to novice snow and ice climbers, as it depends on angling the foot by twisting the ankle so as to keep the whole crampon in contact with the ice. It is best learned on easy slopes, with slow progression onto steeper ground. Experts can negotiate surprisingly steep slopes quickly and safely using French technique.

The feet are kept flat on the ground, in an open-footed stance to prevent crampons snagging on clothing. You do not have to 'stamp' the crampons in – they bite easily under body weight in all but the hardest water ice.

Knees must be bent, the ankles and knees being flexed away from the uphill slope, and the axe being used for balance. Very steep slopes are not easy to negotiate with French technique; diagonals are used.

FRENCH TECHNIQUE

As the slope steepens, so you learn to 'cross over' – the outside foot is placed in front of and slightly higher than the inside foot, and the inside foot then steps higher than the outside, and so on. The common method is to take two steps, move the axe, and step off again. To turn to a new zigzag angle on the diagonal ascent, you lean onto the axe, and 'duck foot' around.

As the gradient increases, you turn your toes more and more down the slope, and the strain becomes greater. It might be necessary to use the axe *à piolet* – with the handle across the body, and the spike driven into the snow at your side, you 'lean' into the ice.

When descending, you face directly down the fall line. The feet are kept flat, allowing all crampon points to bite. The axe is used as a walking stick. This is a very strenuous method and the thighs take a good deal of strain. As the slope steepens, so a diagonal approach may have to be used or even reverse front-pointing.

Front pointing was developed by German and Austrian climbers in the Western Alps. It is better suited to steep ice than the French technique, but needs a good deal of practice to allow for confident movement. Essentially simple, you kick the front points of the crampons into the ice, and then step up on them, using the axes for balance or traction. Placing the points securely is best done with a series of moderate kicks rather than one hard one; the latter can bruise toes after a while.

It is essential that the foot is kept horizontal – the natural tendency is to raise the heel, which forces the crampon points out of their placement, as does leaning into the slope. Staying on vertical balance is ultimately less tiring; it also keeps the maximum amount of contact between the crampon points and the ice. The feet should be about hip width apart. Shorter, more frequent steps are considerably less tiring than large ones.

A combination of the top foot front pointing and the lower foot French pointing can be very effective on moderately steep slopes. This combination is referred to as American technique.

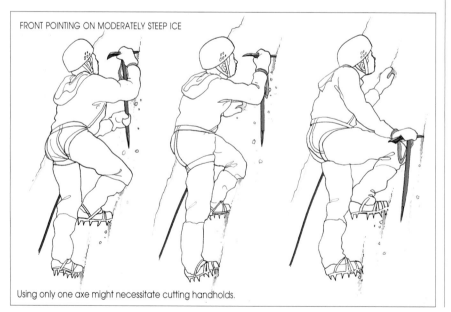

FRONT POINTING ON MODERATELY STEEP ICE

Using only one axe might necessitate cutting handholds.

A climber using two advanced technical axes while bridging on steep, delicate ice.

USING AXES

The ice axe becomes the handhold on steep ice. It is usual to use two axes on steep ground, with one often having an adze and one a hammer. Because of the limitations of short axes on glaciers, moderate ice is often climbed with a short hammer, the longer walking axe being used as the second tool. More severe routes may need two technical axes.

Skilled ice climbers waste little energy, using the weight of the axe to maximum advantage, and gauging the length of their swing to the quality of the ice. Overdriving a pick wastes energy, and can damage fragile ice, as well as making pick removal difficult. Beginners inevitably overdrive, underestimating the security that can be offered by only a centimetre of pick embedded in good ice!

Ice climbing on long, open slopes often demands no more than a consistent rhythm: place the first pick well above the head, then the second; step up one foot, then the next; repeat the small upward steps until the tools are level with your shoulders (*see* illustration below). Repeat again and again... remember, the legs do most of the effort.

On more vertical ice, the arms do more work. Wrist loops are crucial, taking a good deal of the load. Feet and tools are placed slightly further apart.

Where rock abuts the ice, it is common practice to use the axes to torque into cracks or to hook over flakes. This technique can provide rapid and secure upward movement.

CLIMBING WITH AXES

Long leashes can be useful in belays.

Ice climbing demands steadiness, balance, and boldness. Worth remembering is that it is extremely difficult to climb down ice, and thus retreat can be all but impossible. Ensure that you have the resources – mental, physical and equipment – before attempting an ice route.

ICE PROTECTION

Ice screws can offer extremely solid protection points in good ice. They are most secure when placed at an angle of 100 degrees to the slope. Loose ice or snow might have to be cleaned off the surface to ensure a solid placement; the head of the peg should lie flush with the ice, with the eye pointing downhill. If it is impossible to drive the screw in fully, tie it off with a sling close to the ice to minimize leverage.

Most ice screws are screw-in, screw-out. These are started by a light tap with the hammer, then screwed in. Removing them might also involve a hammer tap to loosen the threads which bind with the ice. Using the pick or ferrule, an axe can be used as a lever to set or remove stubborn ice screws. The core of ice

generated in the hollow pegs must be removed before re-use. Body heat might have to be used if the core has frozen in place; blowing into the tube can loosen it (but watch out for lips sticking to the tube!). In insecure ice, it may help to cut a small 'step' in which to place the screw vertically. When ice 'dinner plates' – a round chunk breaks away from the surface as the peg is driven in – it is often best to place the peg in the ice beneath the fallen section, which is less likely to break away again.

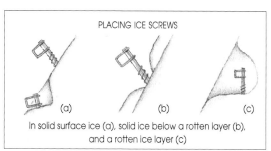

PLACING ICE SCREWS

In solid surface ice (a), solid ice below a rotten layer (b), and a rotten ice layer (c)

Ice-screw threads are created in hard ice by placing and removing tubular screws in such a way that the holes made connect at 45 degrees to the ice face. Rope or tape is then threaded through this (a hooked wire is invaluable). This can provide a fairly secure anchor, particularly for abseils.

Natural ice protections include ice bollards (which can be cut in much the same way as snow bollards), icicles and ice pillars.

Ice axes constitute an excellent back-up form of protection on stances, and are used to allow the leader to rest or hang while placing protection.

SNOW AND ICE ABSEILS

The only differences to rock abseils are that the rope may be frozen and difficult to handle, and the abseil points more marginal. A slow, steady descent is wise.

If abseiling off a snow or ice bollard, tie a sling rather than the rope around the bollard, as under pressure the rope may freeze into the bollard.

It is possible to use ice screws and ice axes in such a way that they can be recovered. It is worth practising this thoroughly, as you neither want them to come loose of their own accord when you are half-way down the slope, nor stick forever far above you!

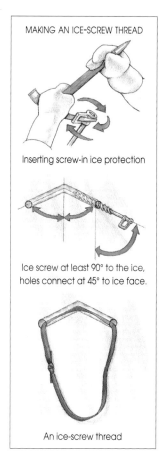

MAKING AN ICE-SCREW THREAD

Inserting screw-in ice protection

Ice screw at least 90° to the ice, holes connect at 45° to ice face.

An ice-screw thread

Left Soloing up a frozen waterfall to the start of the real ice route.

Opposite Climbing steep waterfall ice demands a delicate technique.

BACKING UP ICE SCREWS WITH AXES

Right and far right Powder-snow avalanches can have devastating effects.

To negotiate this typical alpine cornice, the climber should stay well back from the edge.

AVALANCHES, CORNICES, SÉRACS AND OTHER SNOW AND ICE HAZARDS

Delightful as snow and ice can be, they are also fraught with dangers. Avalanches represent the number one danger to snow travellers. Evaluating the stability of a snow pack is a highly technical and still much-debated skill. Guidelines are given below, but this is not sufficient for full snow analyses. Seek local, expert advice, and make sure that you avoid avalanche-prone areas.

Eighty per cent of avalanches strike during or just after snowstorms, with danger increasing if the fall has exceeded 2cm (¾in) per hour, and at its greatest if accumulated snow has built up to 30cm (1ft) or more. Rapid changes in temperature after storms, particularly rises, can increase the hazards.

SNOW AND AVALANCHES

Snow is essentially crystallized water, formed high in the atmosphere when cooling water droplets begin to solidify around minute dust particles. The now heavy snowflake starts to fall, and to grow – by sublimation (more water vapour is deposited on the crystal), or riming (further small water droplets freeze onto the crystal). Snow crystals form in roughly hexagonal shapes.

Snowflakes are constantly altered as they pass through the cycle from formation back to water or water vapour, and then back to formation. It is these changes and their results on snow-pack conditions that affect the climber.

Equitemperature (ET) Metamorphism is where snow crystals under pressure go from pretty branched shapes to rounded blobs found in low-temperature (subzero) snow packs. The branching arms of adjacent crystals unlink, leading to snow with low cohesion. Then, if the temperature stays low, the snow once again relinks. Powder skiing, for instance, only becomes excellent a relatively short while after a snowfall – about 24 hours. It is seldom wise to climb or ski directly after a snowfall.

Temperature-gradient (TG) Metamorphism, which is characterized by the formation of cup crystals, is a condition which leads to great avalanche potential. This occurs when shallowish snow lies on ground that is warmer than the snow surface. Water vapour moves through the snow pack, slowly forming cup crystals in the layers. Further snowfalls lead to layers of soft, crumbly snow on harder layers, with the cup crystals acting as 'ball bearings' and producing a shear plane (plane of breakage). This, in turn, can lead to wind-slab avalanches.

Melt-freeze (MF) Metamorphism is the more usual weathering of snow caused by alternate above- and below-zero temperatures. This causes crystals to first shrink and form thin water layers, and then refreeze. A stable, compact snow pack is produced.

SNOW TYPES

Powder snow: loose snow, found under 0°C (32°F) with little wind. Subject to ET metamorphism, this can lead to avalanche conditions before it reconsolidates (days or weeks). If deep, it is difficult and tiring to move through, requiring a 'wading' technique.
Wind slab: where falling snow or already deposited snow is picked up by wind and redeposited. The crystals are smashed, and often relink on impact. The stronger the wind, the harder the slab. Wind slab makes up most mountain snow .
Névé: is a climber's dream; hard enough to support the climber, soft enough for crampon penetration. It is stable, and formed by MF metamorphism. It is

The formation known as 'névé penitente' can make progress difficult, sometimes creating 'pinnacles' over a metre high.

well-aerated snow, and therefore 'crumbly but firm'.

It is the combination of prevailing snow types and conditions of formation which influences avalanche potential. Ridges and buttresses offer safer ground; gullies and couloirs (larger gullies) are risky. Wind-swept crests often lead to snow build-up just past the ridge, which may lead to a wind slab avalanche.

Correct   Incorrect

THE MOST SUITABLE ROUTE TO MINIMIZE THE RISK OF AN AVALANCHE

AVALANCHE POTENTIAL

If the bonds between the layers of snow or the snow and the ground weaken, then the snow will slide if on a slope. The only safe way to assess snow conditions is to dig a snow profile every so often – a laborious task. The best snow profiles go all the way to the ground, although this may be impractical. The danger is greatest if there are alternating hard and soft layers with a thick, soft layer on top of a hard one.

Hardness is graded from 1 (can push a gloved fist in – powder snow) to 5 (needs force with an ice pick to penetrate – consolidated névé). If there is a difference of 3 or above between adjacent layers, it is dangerous. Wetness also plays a role – wet, heavy, lubricated snow slides more easily. Dry snow (wetness 1) cannot form snowballs, wet snow (5) allows water to be squeezed out of it.

The presence of the 'ball-bearing' cup crystals (seen as a rice-like 'crumbly' snow) in a mid or lower layer enhances avalanche risk. The angle of ground also plays a role – most avalanches occur on slopes of 30 to 45 degrees; convex slopes put the snow under tension, leading to avalanches breaking off. **Wind-slab avalanches** are the most common. Wind slab, at its worst, 'squeaks' when walked on. It has a fine, smooth surface texture, and is dull rather than shiny. High temperatures cause an inter-layer melt, and the slab moves. Often it takes little more than a loud noise or a single step to trigger the disintegration of the weak inter-layer bonds.

Powder-snow avalanches, occurring soon after heavy snow falls, can be devastating, with huge volumes of fine snow pushing walls of air before them. These occur most frequently in the Himalayas.

Wet-snow avalanches are often presaged by small snowballs running down the slopes. They occur when the temperature rises above zero, often in the late afternoon. Any rapid rise in temperature should give rise to extreme caution in avalanche-prone areas.

AVALANCHE SURVIVAL

Being avalanched does not mean certain death. Running up an avalanching slope, 'swimming', or rolling sideways or to the surface can minimize the amount of snow covering you. As the avalanche slows down, try to swim to the surface if you have some orientation.

As a last ditch effort, burrow around to clear a breathing space around you before the pack starts to consolidate. Try to avoid panic, as you need to conserve oxygen. Only shout if you can clearly hear someone shouting at you.

Rescue

The witness to an avalanche can make all the difference to the victim's chances of survival. Watch carefully to see the track of the victim. Move down the line connecting the start of the climber's slide and the position the victim was last seen in. Search immediately, probing with axes, ski-poles or tent poles. Shout, but allow listening times. If you find the victim, and he is not conscious, clear snow from his mouth and attempt artificial resuscitation immediately, i.e. before even digging him entirely clear of the snow. The first 15 minutes are crucial to survival, although victims of avalanches have been recovered alive after quite a few hours. Avalanche beacons can be invaluable – if you are wearing these, then use them as outlined in their manuals.

ICE

Eventually most snow packs will form ice. The quality of the ice will depend on its method of formation, the angle of slope, and any extra material that may be incorporated in it, such as glacial silt. Séracs and ice falls occur when there are large temperature changes; ice is usually stable in the cold early mornings and nights.

CORNICES

These overhanging snow masses tend to form at ridges or crests as a result of wind action. They can be huge and are often far more undercut than their appearance suggests – many a climber has been taken by crumbling cornices. A line leading well below the crest of ridges must be taken, as cornices are prone to break off far back from the vertical line of the ridge.

Opposite A stable crevasse provides a sheltered rest spot. The climbers are sitting well clear of hanging icicles. Nose shields on sunglasses protect these climbers against the harsh effects of ultraviolet rays at high altitude.

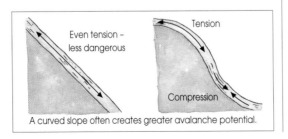

A curved slope often creates greater avalanche potential.

WHERE TO SEARCH FOR AN AVALANCHE VICTIM
Point **a** indicates where the avalanche started (note break
off wall above); point **b** indicates the last place where
the victim was seen; therefore, the most likely place
to find the victim is in the area marked **c**.

If approaching from below, it is usually best to
traverse a long way to avoid them, although passing
below a fragile cornice can constitute quite a danger
in itself. Often you have to tunnel through the cornice. In this case, it is best to have the belayer off to
one side in case of a break-off of the cornice.

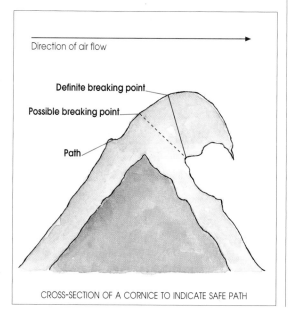

CROSS-SECTION OF A CORNICE TO INDICATE SAFE PATH

CHAPTER EIGHT

ALPINE CLIMBING
The Speed Merchants

The European Alps were the foremost playground for mountaineers around the turn of the century, during the Golden Years of climbing. Since then, many other alpine-style areas have been pioneered such as New Zealand, North America and Canada, parts of South America, and even Africa. For the purposes of this book, alpine climbing is essentially taken to imply one-day ascents comprising mixed rock, ice and snow climbs, where the party carries all gear, with no prestocked sub-camps. Alpine-style ascents are even made on 8000m (26,250ft) Himalayan peaks over a number of days, but the principle of self-sufficiency remains.

Speed is of the essence in alpine climbing – to succeed on a route of any complexity, the party must be capable of moving together rapidly over mixed terrain. Alpine climbing thus ideally requires a pair or party which is well-matched in their climbing ability and which has a fair degree of experience. It combines all the joys but also all of the hazards of both rock climbing, and snow and ice climbing – and in addition to these it requires sound movement, navigation and route-finding skills.

Ladders are useful in crossing large crevasses; note safety line.

PREPARATION FOR ALPINE CLIMBING

The alpinist should be well-versed in all of the principles and practices of rock as well as snow and ice climbing. It might seem a little juvenile to practise crevasse rescue on dry ground or off a cliff face at the local crag; however, it will pay off should

The Karakorum in Pakistan has some superb alpine and super-alpine climbing venues.

you ever need to apply it. Similarly, moving roped together over easy rock is better learned in a familiar environment than on an easy but exposed alpine ridge at 04:00, with the effects of high altitude and cold creating additional hazards.

Alpinism can be learned from scratch by a pair of novices entirely on their own, but trying this could prove hazardous without sufficient time being allowed to progress from simple glacier walks via short climbs to more ambitious objectives. Making use of one of the many competent alpine guides or climbing schools to gain the necessary skills and experience is a good idea. Particularly if one has limited time, the expense is amply justified.

Taking refuge in an ice shelter.

Above The approach to the climb may involve a long and arduous hike, often through spectacular scenery.

Opposite left Both climbers and equipment must be securely tied on to a bivouac ('bivvy') ledge.

When in a new area, it is best to attempt alpine routes which are ostensibly a few grades lower than your normal standard, as the familiarization process takes time and often brings some surprises. The effects of altitude should not be forgotten either – a TD-grade (*see* page 152) route at 3500m (11,500ft) and 5°C (40°F) with an alpine pack is a different proposition to the same grade at sea level, without a pack, on a warm summer's day. Initially you should choose a route with stable, predictable conditions, so as to reduce the potential problems.

Unlike the average day at the crag, an alpine route of any magnitude will require thorough pre-planning. This may include:
• Determining the best season or time of year.
• Studying of topos and route descriptions, to the extent of making a summarized copy in a waterproof or plastic covering.

• Doing an easy neighbouring route in order to take a closer look at your objective and establish descent routes when not under pressure.
• Checking equipment, both personal (always remembering the possibility of a bivouac or emergency situation) and climbing gear; both ice and rock gear might be required. A compromise between weight and speed is often needed – too much or too little equipment might jeopardize your safety (being either underequipped or overloaded).
• Scouting approach routes, including the most suitable hut or base (or bivouac) from which to depart.
• Ascertaining escape and descent routes, including grid references and compass bearings in the event of mist, rain or snow.
• Checking weather forecasts and projections.
• Checking snow conditions and route conditions with others who have recently been in the vicinity.

ALPINE EQUIPMENT

A mix of snow and rock gear often has to be carried, depending on the route. Gear must be dependable and as light as possible. Generally, modern gear is extremely lightweight – without sacrificing strength or function.

In most cases, only the approach and parts of the descent are undertaken over a glacier or on snow and ice, with the majority of the climb taking place on rock. Each climber would normally have:

• A rucksack of at least 35-litre (62-pint) capacity, with body-contouring features
• A layered clothing system (*see* Chapter Seven); plastic boots and crampons with snow gaiters; a balaclava; sunglasses; a helmet; and thin and thicker outer gloves
• A pair of rock boots if there is a lot of technical rock (for alpine use it is wise to have a looser pair than usual to wear with socks for warmth)
• Either a walking axe or a pair of technical axes depending on route severity

• Some sort of bivouac bag for emergencies
• A headtorch with spare batteries and bulbs
• A waterbottle
• Some snack food (e.g. cheese, chocolate).

In general, for a typical longish mixed alpine route each pair would carry:
• Two 9mm ropes
• A rock rack consisting of a mixture of camming devices in medium-size range, a set of nuts, a few short slings (e.g. quickdraws) and a few longer ones (for tying off ice screws and axes or extending runners)
• Four or five ice screws
• One or two deadmen
• A detailed map, compass and often an altimeter – useful for checking both weather patterns and altitude
• A few metres of nylon webbing tape for descent abseils, with a knife to cut it
• A small first-aid kit
• A repair kit for crampons, etc.

Hanging storm cooker

Popular additions include a stainless steel thermos flask for hot drinks, adjustable ski-poles for the walk in and out, and packs with a built-in water bladder for constant hydration.

If a bivouac is likely, then a stove, a pot and matches, some extra food, and a bivouac bag must be added to the list. A small down sleeping bag or extra anorak and trousers might also be included.

Once again the main problem of alpine climbing emerges: what must you take as a safe minimum of equipment and what must you leave to save weight and enhance speed and efficiency of movement? By taking just too much, the alpinist may compromise speed and end up having to use all of the bivouac gear taken. By taking too little they may, despite the extra speed gained, end up spending a dangerously exposed night out as a result of a storm or unexpected delay.

To some extent this is determined by the experience of the party plus the nature of the route, and ultimately by the boldness and the commitment of the climbers. There is no fail-safe formula.

A warm drink and a bar of chocolate – a climber's lifesavers.

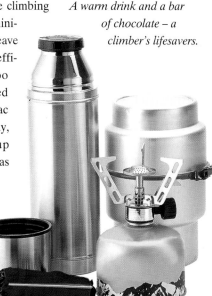

Right Facilities at mountain huts range from the basic to the luxurious.

Below Flipping pancakes in a cozy ice cave.

SPECIALIST ALPINE TECHNIQUES

THE APPROACH

Huts are an integral part of the proud tradition of mountaineering, and are found – in some surprising places – in most alpine areas. They vary from simple emergency shelters to virtual hotels. If unattended, respect the ethos and environment of the hut, and leave it in the condition you found it (or better). In attended huts, the wardens are boss, and can make or break your stay (financially or in terms of the best sleeping locations!). They are often highly experienced climbers themselves and their advice is ignored at your peril.

Being a member of a Mountain Club which has reciprocal rights through the UIAA can often lead to big reductions in hut fees. Always carry membership cards with attached photographs. Many hut wardens prefer the fees to be paid in advance – a wise precaution on their part.

Alpine approaches involve early starts and a few tips can make life considerably easier:

• Alpine huts are busy places, and get horribly crowded in season. For popular huts (i.e. most

European huts) book ahead to avoid disappointment and a bitterly cold night spent huddled in your emergency bivvy bag. Check on dates of operation if it is early or late in the season.

• Hut wardens will generally provide hot water for no or little extra cost; this helps if self-catering. Many huts in the European Alps are almost of five-star hotel standard and meals, drinks, etc., can usually be purchased. Most allow cooking and some even provide cooking services for no extra charge. It is advisable to enquire in advance.

• Blankets are usually provided in the bigger huts, so there is no need to carry a bulky sleeping bag. A light pertex or similar inner sheet provides peace of mind and comfort.

• Don't expect a good night's sleep unless you are impervious to noise – hut occupants start going to bed at 17:00 or so, and leave at all hours. Remember that climbers will be getting up at midnight to take advantage of the good frozen ice and snow or because of the length of the route. Some hardy souls simply don't go to sleep, and party noisily on until departure time or fiddle jinglingly with gear for hours on end, crinkling the noisiest plastic bags you have ever heard. There are the inevitable snorers and groaners or the restless souls who dig you in the side as they flail around.

• Earplugs are useful – but make sure that someone will wake you!

• If you like fresh air, sleep near a window, but expect an ongoing battle between those who want it closed and those who want it open.

• For your own, and everyone else's sake, pack fully before going to bed. By having everything ready you will streamline your departure and not have to grovel around looking for your gear in the midst of the

Bottom left In good conditions you can bivouac almost anywhere, provided you have the right equipment.

Bottom right Much-needed insulation and an escape from dripping melt-ice is provided by erecting a tent inside a snow-cave.

Opposite bottom left Crowds in the Vallée Blanche illustrate the pressure on the mountain environment.

Opposite right Expedition flags wave over the tents of Advance Base Camp, Annapurna, Nepal.

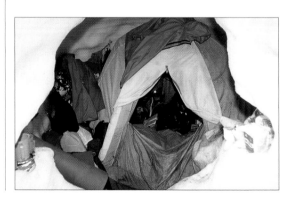

chaos of 20 others, many of whom will be total incompetents with their long-suffering guides.

• It might not be fashionable, but marking your gear with bright, distinctive colours helps you to avoid wearing somebody else's boots or Goretex top. Choosing ugly, unfashionable colours also reduces the chance of theft – which is sadly becoming more prevalent in today's climbing society.

• Ensure that your torch is easily accessible, and has new batteries to avoid delays in the morning.

• Hydrate well before leaving the hut, and often on the approach march.

BIVOUACS ('BIVVIES')

In many European areas, bivouacking in tents is discouraged or even forbidden at times (for example, in the Vallée Blanche at Chamonix, which is becoming overrun with climbers and their waste during high season). Once again, make enquiries locally to avoid problems.

A bivouac can be as simple as drawing your pack up around you, tied to a belay on a tiny sloping ledge, or as luxurious as a comfortable tent in a valley. A stove is essential. For moderate altitudes (i.e. below 6000m; 19,685ft) a propane-butane resealable gas cartridge stove is the most convenient option, although some climbers will swear by their petrol-powered gadgets. Plenty of hot fluids – such as hot chocolate, soup, tea, and so on – constitute the climber's staple diet.

A foam pad provides insulation (many packs have detachable pads inside) and a down jacket or sleeping bag adds to the comfort. Sleeping with your waterbottle, boots and rope may be the only way to ensure that they are useable the next morning and not frozen into solid lumps.

GETTING TO THE ROUTE

As you will probably be doing this in the dark it helps to reconnoitre even the first part of the route in daylight beforehand. Many parties rope up in the warmth of the hut, and walk roped together to the base of the route. It seldom detracts from speed or enjoyment. Standard roping up (*see* page 121) is used.

Snow and ice conditions are usually most stable in the very early morning, after the cooler night temperatures, stabilizing again in the evening. Many

Top The effects of altitude, even on the 4000m (13,000ft) high European Alps, should not be underestimated. Rope management in this party is somewhat suspect!

Right Sunrise at Santa Cruz, South America, heralds a new day and a new challenge. The normal route follows the obvious line up the gradual spur in the centre.

parties plan their route so as to finish the approach over the snow before daylight, and it is common to start climbing the ice, rock or mixed ground by torchlight, particularly on longer routes.

Some prior knowledge of the route – its starting position at least – is essential. Studying the approach via binoculars (a small, high-quality pair is indispensable) and photographs helps prevent you from being halfway up before realizing at first light that you are on the wrong route!

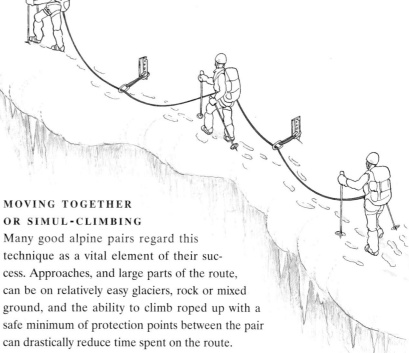

SIMUL-CLIMBING
Here using running belays.

MOVING TOGETHER OR SIMUL-CLIMBING

Many good alpine pairs regard this technique as a vital element of their success. Approaches, and large parts of the route, can be on relatively easy glaciers, rock or mixed ground, and the ability to climb roped up with a safe minimum of protection points between the pair can drastically reduce time spent on the route.

Once again, this is a skill which is best practised on familiar or very easy ground beforehand.

In simul-climbing it is usual to use a rope-length of 10 to 20m (33 to 65ft), depending on the terrain and the belays offered. The leader moves off, with the second following on a fairly taut rope. The leader will indicate that he is placing a runner, both climbers stop, the leader places the gear and both move off. The first protection is only removed by the second once the leader has at least one other piece (preferably two) in between the pair.

When the leader has run out of gear, the second is brought up to the leader on belay, and the lead or gear is exchanged. In this fashion, a pair of good climbers can move over relatively difficult ground very rapidly, but still with a margin of safety. Very often the chosen belay, for purposes of efficiency, is a friction hitch directly onto the belay protection.

The rope alone can be used as an effective means of 'running protection'. On many easy to moderate grade climbs, there can be suitable spikes or rock projections to loop the rope around as the leader climbs past. In many areas of Europe, Via Ferrata – long climbs or traverses protected by cables – offer an easy way to and from summits or harder sections of routes. These are often simul-climbed to speed up progress and avoid having to re-rope the party.

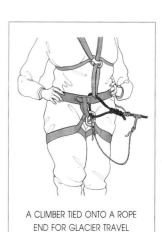

A CLIMBER TIED ONTO A ROPE
END FOR GLACIER TRAVEL
Note prusik loops *in situ*, and
chest harness linked to the rope.

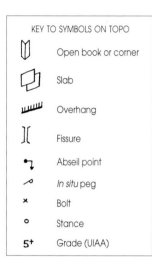
WEATHER

The weather in alpine areas can change rapidly and making use of weather predictions can spell success or disaster. It is often better to sit it out in frustration in the valley for a few days, rather than rush off to do a route in too small a weather gap. Patience and flexibility are essential for a good alpine season.

An altimeter is within the financial reach of most climbing parties. The models on watches, although not as accurate as dedicated instruments, give useful predictions of weather trends.

A falling barometric pressure over a few hours at a fixed location indicates trouble and should be taken seriously.

OBJECTIVE DANGERS

Alpine areas bring dangers which are not shared with lower-level rock climbs or hikes: rock falls, avalanches, crevasses, sérac falls, etc., cannot always be predicted. However, the risks can be cut down by moving at the correct time of day or by choosing a more appropriate route. Alpine climbs start early simply because the snow and ice are frozen during the cool nights, resulting in less chance of stonefall from rocks breaking free of melting ice; crevasse bridges are firmer and avalanche slopes less prone to movement.

Your choice of route, for example, moving on ridges rather than exposed slopes and avoiding convex slopes, can reduce avalanche and stonefall risk further. Risks from lightning are greater if you are in or near a crack system, particularly in the wet. In a severe storm – when your equipment is singing and your hair is standing on end – partial insulation can be obtained by sitting on your pack, away from cracks and the rock face. Remember too that fresh snow on older snow is particularly prone to avalanche until a few days have passed to allow it to consolidate and bind with the lower layers.

Far too often parties blame their mishaps on the weather conditions when, in reality, the blame lies in their inadequate physical or mental preparation, lack of sufficient or appropriate equipment, or poor choice of route.

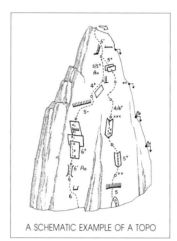

A SCHEMATIC EXAMPLE OF A TOPO

KEEPING TO THE ROUTE
Route descriptions and topos

Many modern route descriptions are done in 'topo form' (i.e. a pictorial representation). Learning to interpret these is useful – it helps to scout out the land with binoculars while referring to a topo of the same area. This will stand you in good stead on an unknown route followed by topo or route description only.

ROPE MANAGEMENT

Effective rope management is useful in all types of climbing, but essential in alpinism. A rope carelessly coiled at the top of a climb can spell tragedy as a cold, exhausted climber struggles to undo it for abseil; a poorly handled rope which snakes down from a tiny belay ledge can snag on spikes below or bring down rockfall on a second. A useful technique on a small belay ledge is to practise coiling the rope over your feet to keep it close at hand and tidy.

THE DESCENT

Many descents in alpine areas involve abseils at some point, thus long slings to back up existing pegs or for use as primary abseil slings are vital. Most parties carry 10 to 12m (33 to 40ft) of tape or cord to cut up for this. Carrying a small amount of spectra cord for abseils over sharp edges is recommended, as it is far more resistant to wear and tear than ordinary tape or rope.

Once off the rock, good map-and-compass work can be vital, particularly if it has started to snow or cloud over or if darkness has set in. An altimeter helps to locate traverse levels, passes and cols.

Many parties come to grief on the descent, as they are tired and errors of judgement can occur more readily than on the ascent. Parties should watch one another, and look for signs of exhaustion or hypothermia. Not stopping to take a sip of liquid or chunk of chocolate, or to pull on the outer shell jacket, could spell disaster.

Remember – your climb is not over until every climber is safely 'home'.

Above *Patagonia's Towers of Paine are favoured for extreme alpine-style expeditions.*

Left *An easy ridge approach to the Tour Ronde, part of the French Alps.*

ALPINISM AND EMERGENCIES

Because of their committing nature, alpine routes breed emergencies. Anyone who has spent a few days at Chamonix in high season will be familiar with the incessant to-ing and fro-ing of the dragonfly-like rescue helicopters.

Being prepared to cope with common emergencies could save lives. Remember that being calm helps both the rescued and the rescuer, and that unnecessary haste can cause further complications. Above all, take care not to compromise the safety of the rest of the party at the expense of the injured party – no 'false heroics'.

Overleaf An avalanche approaches Everest Base Camp, Khumbu Glacier.

Right A large expedition at their Bolivian base camp.

EXPEDITIONS

For many climbers, expeditions are the culmination of many years of dreaming and planning, the 'cherry on the top' of the climbing cake. In essence, the climbing techniques themselves on any expedition do not vary greatly from those described in the other chapters of the book. However, the time frame is longer, the logistics become more complicated, and the effects of altitude and weather more significant.

In a larger-scale expedition, the rules of the game also change somewhat: the objective is to put at least one of the team on the summit and usually no means are considered 'foul' (except perhaps the use of helicopters).

You should choose an objective within the anticipated climbing ability of the party, taking into account the unsettling effects of altitude. The time available to the team is also of great significance as climbs always seem to take longer than initially projected.

The **climbing area** is of prime importance – good expedition areas can be found in the Himalayas, Karakorum (Kashmir), Pamirs (central Asia), Alaska, Patagonia, other parts of the Andes, Russia, and more remote places such as Greenland, Antarctica, and the subantarctic island of South Georgia. Africa and New Zealand also offer expedition possibilities.

PREPARATION

Organizing a sizable expedition involves scores of minute details, from ensuring the expedition has sufficient shoelaces to booking air tickets. Some areas that need consideration are:

• **Climbing style:** is it a 'full siege', with fixed ropes, many sub-camps, porters and the like; or an alpine-style, lightweight push? The former needs a structured 'pyramid' approach to supplies, with quantities tapering off as the group moves to higher sub-camps.

• **Food:** variety is the key, and eating local food on the approach march makes the prepacked high-altitude food more appealing later on. Most expedition diets work on a mix of 50% carbohydrate, 30% fat and 20% protein. Avoid overcatering in bad weather or when conditions delay the climb – the food must be made to last.

• **Water** is untrustworthy in most of the world so a suitable filter can be a genuine lifesaver! Boiling is not a guaranteed way of purifying water, particularly at altitude where water boils at such a low temperature that many organisms can still survive. Iodine and chlorine are good antibacterials, although some micro-organisms are resistant to them. The best advice is to boil, treat and filter all water.

• **Fuel and stoves:** gas stoves are the most convenient and least fiddly option (important under the stresses of high altitude). A propane-butane mix which works adequately at surprisingly high altitudes is available for most popular models, but canisters are seldom to be found in Third World areas.

Above and below Packing and sorting are a key element of expeditions.

Clarifying the objective is vital as it determines the structure and nature of the expedition:

• Is the peak snow-covered?

• Does it require rock/ice/mixed climbing?

• At what altitude are the difficulties?

• How close can you get by road?

• Is it a first ascent or is the route well-documented?

• Are sub-camps needed?

• What dangers are there (glaciers, crevasses, avalanches, loose rock)?

• What are the prevailing weather patterns?

• What is the most favourable time of year?

• How large a team is needed for success?

• Are porters needed and, if so, are they available?

• How much will the entire expedition cost?

For base camp, ordinary pressurized primus-type kerosene or paraffin stoves are dependable and 'porter friendly'; they are virtually indestructible. Fuel is readily available in most parts of the world. Alcohol is an essential primer.

Multi-fuel stoves which take benzine, petrol, and almost anything that burns are suitable for advanced base camps and even higher. Remember, however, that they have a tendency to block and can be somewhat fiddly. Cold, numb hands and brains do not enjoy trying to figure out the complexities of intricate, tiny stove parts at 7500m (24,600ft). This is where gas stoves come into their own.

Take a good fuel filter, and filter all fuel.

• **Group equipment:** a hoard of specialized and nonspecialized kit is needed for any major expedition.

Here are some useful hints:

Things fail. Take a comprehensive repair kit with tools including pliers, a vice-grip, file, and screwdrivers. Duct tape holds most things together so take plenty, as well as wire and strong nylon cord of about 4mm (0.2in) thickness. Take a sewing kit, including heavy-duty needles and nylon cord for tent and other repairs; tent-pole splices (or a few spare poles); extra stove and crampon parts; patch kits for air mattresses; and spare pack buckles.

• **Training:** the team needs to train, individually and, if possible, together. The best training is climbing, with good long walk-ins to assist cardiovascular conditioning.

A higher than usual standard of climbing fitness is normally required before expeditions, where travel delays and high-altitude stresses can quickly sap your reserves.

Mental conditioning is crucial. This comes from the team working together, particularly if the team does some hard, taxing climbs in preparation for the expedition.

THE CLIMB

Assuming that your expedition takes you to high altitudes, be aware of the need for slow, purposeful acclimatization. The walk-in to base camp can often help to solve this problem if taken slowly, allowing time for the body to adapt. The body needs exertion at altitude to acclimatize, but also needs rest days at lower altitudes. Above 6000m (9690ft) deterioration sets in regardless of pre-acclimatization, and this intensifies the higher you go. Try to minimize stays at high altitudes.

Both alpine-style and pyramid-style ascents need careful planning; the supply of food and equipment up a route needs a logical and systematic approach. The sensible leader commits things to paper and does not rely on mind and memory alone. Very often it is useful to have a 'base camp manager', who does not commit himself to the high-altitude climbing and can thus keep a clear head for logistics.

RETURNING

Some climbers think that a climb ends once the top of the route is reached. In reality, the expedition only ends when all the team members are safely down. The danger of pushing things just too far in order to reach the goal becomes even more real at altitude, where your reasoning powers are severely diminished.

Expedition climbing is certainly about pushing the limits, about testing yourself and the team in a very severe situation; however, each person and team must decide what level of risk and commitment they wish to make. No summit is worth the sacrifice of a life.

Adhering to turn-around times can be difficult, but if the team has decided on this, then it should be drummed into all the members. After all, as Reinhold Messner put it: 'The whole object of mountaineering is to come back to talk about it'.

THE HUNT FOR ADVENTURE

Although all of the major peaks have been climbed, there are still new challenges awaiting those with the enthusiasm to try for a new route on an already climbed peak, or hunt out one of the yet-unclimbed peaks in the Andes, Himalayas or elsewhere.

A safe return from the summit of Everest.

BASIC NAVIGATION

At some stage any active climber or mountaineer will find himself crossing new ground, be it on approach or retreat. Confidence and competence in the use of a map and compass is vital and can only really come with practice. Trusting the compass and your own ability in a whiteout (diminished vision due to mist or snow) or at night in a storm is not easy, and many a party have found themselves in trouble due to their inability to use the basic tools of navigation.

This section is a very brief introduction to an important and complex element of mountaineering which needs intensive study and regular practice to achieve proficiency.

Rotating bezel with compass (protractor)

0° or North indicator

North end of the magnetic needle

Roamer scale

Direction of travel arrow

MAPS

Modern relief/contour maps give a good idea of the profile of the country. However, ordinary contour (topographic) maps give the same information to a skilled navigator.

A useful scale is 1:50,000 (1 unit on the map = 50,000 of these units on the ground, e.g. 1cm = 50,000cm, or 500m; 1in = 50,000in, or about 4165ft).

Apart from features such as roads, buildings, rivers and vegetation, the key element to any topographical map is the **contour line**. Each line represents a particular constant elevation. The **contour interval** is the vertical height rise represented by each successive line – this is usually about 10 or 20m (40 or 80ft on US maps). Major contour lines are printed darker and labelled with the height somewhere along their length. The closer together the contour lines, the steeper the slope.

A useful tip is to keep maps in plastic bags or special map cases, or to laminate them. A soggy mass of wet paper will not be of great help in escaping from a tricky situation.

Navigating by Map Alone

Most navigation is actually done without constant reference to the compass. The map is orientated using the compass (*see* diagrams A and B opposite), then the map is matched to features on the ground. In general this is sufficient to allow you to navigate to the destination, perhaps with occasional checks of the compass against the map to confirm orientation.

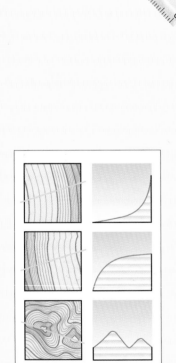

RELIEF MAP SECTIONS
(Top to bottom): a concave slope; a convex slope; and two summits separated by a col.

Take note that most maps show both **magnetic north** and **true north**. (*See* 'magnetic variation', opposite.)

The map must be aligned to the ground on true north, but should be aligned to the compass needle using magnetic north.

NAVIGATING BY MAP AND COMPASS

In extreme conditions, or in bad visibility, the map features alone may not suffice. The climber must then navigate using advanced skills, with the compass playing a large role.

The **compass** is essentially a simple device, but one fraught with problems for the untrained. One fallacy is that it always points north. Yes, it should, but compasses respond to all magnetic fields and iron objects. Beware of metal objects in your pockets (or even metal spectacle frames if using a 'sighting compass'), torches and batteries in night navigation, watches, ice axes, and even some metallic areas of the earth's crust.

Compasses have a seldom-recognized 'dip' factor called **magnetic inclination** (as opposed to the more familiar variation – *see* opposite) which affects the horizontal alignment of the needle. A compass needle 'weighted' for the far northern hemisphere may 'stick' to the base of the compass near the equator or in the southern hemisphere, resulting in incorrect navigation. Check that you have an appropriate compass.

The most useful compass for navigation has a rotating bezel on a transparent base plate, with a direction-of-travel arrow marked on it. These compasses usually have graduated scales called roamer scales, which enable you to measure distances on the map. Many have a number of different roamers to take into account a range of map scales.

When travelling from one point to another you may sometimes follow a simple heading such as 'due north' or 'directly west'. However, navigation is very seldom this straightforward and considerable accuracy is required, for example, if you are heading for a small neck or pass through thick mist at night. In circumstances like this, you have to use **bearings**.

The compass circle is divided into the familiar 360°, with north being at 0°, east 90°, south 180°, and west 270°. These numbers are referred to as bearings. Experienced navigators can be accurate to within a few metres over large distances.

The compass is used for two functions. One is to *take bearings*, either by sighting along the compass from your position to a distant point (e.g. a distant hill) or by measuring a bearing from one point to another on a map (see diagrams A and B opposite).

The other function is to *plot or follow bearings*. This is when the compass is set to a particular bearing, either by taking sightings along the compass or via measurement on the map. That bearing is followed on the ground or on the map to arrive at a point (*see* diagrams C to E opposite).

BEARINGS ON THE MAP

The compass is used here as a simple protractor and the magnetic needle need not be involved at all (the map does not necessarily have to be orientated to north). Bearings for escape routes from obvious points on the climb can be plotted at home beforehand using the map and compass-protractor.

To plot a bearing from point X to point Y

• Place the compass on the map so that one long edge runs between points X and Y (*see* diagram C).

• Check that the direction-of-travel arrow points to Y.

• Turn the rotating bezel so that the N–S line parallels the 'true' N–S lines on the map (a conventional map is set to 'true' N–S). (*See* diagram D.)

• Read the number on the index line (direction-of-travel line). This is the bearing from X to Y (in this example, 340°). (*See* diagram E.)

Converting this to a usable bearing on the ground

You are now at point X, in the dark, and wish to get to Y. If you set 340° onto the direction-of-travel line on your compass, and then followed this, you would not end up at Y! The reason for this is **magnetic variation** (also called magnetic declination). The **magnetic** North Pole is unfortunately **not** the same as the **true** North Pole, around which the earth rotates on its axis. Depending on where you are on earth, the needle is a greater or smaller degree off true North. This figure is always given on the map as magnetic variation.

Left of the 0° (Greenwich meridian) line, the figure is, for example, -10°. This figure is subtracted from the bearing of 340° obtained above. You would then walk on a magnetic bearing of 330° to get from X to Y.

If you were **right of the 0° line**, and the variation was +10°, you would add it to 340°, giving a compass or magnetic bearing of 350°.

Check the information on the map: it will normally read as 'Magnetic variation: 15°E', for example. This means: 'go 15° further east of your true bearing' i.e. **add** 15°. If it said '15°W', then you would **subtract** 15°, i.e. go further west.

TO FOLLOW A BEARING ON THE GROUND

• Set the bearing from the map as above, taking into account magnetic variation. For example:

$$340° + (or -) 15° \text{ variation} = 355° (or 325°)$$

The rotating dial must thus have 355° (or 325°) on the direction-of-travel arrow.

• Hold the compass level in front of you and turn it (and your body) until the north needle of the compass lines up with the north arrow on the rotating dial. (*See* diagram E.)

• The direction-of-travel arrow now indicates the way to go. Follow this direction.

MORE ADVANCED SKILLS IN FOLLOWING MAP AND COMPASS

In bad conditions, it is easy to lose track of where you are even using a map and compass. **Maintaining direction** can be done by sighting along the line of travel and identifying a feature, e.g. a prominent rock, on that line. Head for this feature, then resight to the next visible feature. If the terrain is featureless, 'leapfrog' by sending a climber ahead, getting them in line, placing another beyond them, then leapfrogging to the front and repeating this. Usually this process is rather time-consuming, so it is often better simply to keep on checking the compass, and maintain direction as best you can. **You must trust the compass.**

Keeping track of the distance travelled can be useful. By measuring the distance from X to Y on the map, you can then use the scale to work out the actual distance on the ground.

For example:

If X to Y = 2.5cm on the map, which has a scale of 1:20,000, then the distance on the ground is:

$$2.5 \times 20,000 = 50,000cm$$
$$\div 100 \ (100cm=1m) = 500m$$

If you know your pace length (it is advisable to work this out in advance while practising navigation) then you can count paces (often 2 paces = 1m in difficult terrain). You can also work on time: the average party under difficult conditions walks at approximately 3kph = 3000m/60 minutes = 50m per minute. Thus, 500m should take about 10 minutes. This gives you some idea as to when you expect to reach Y. If after 10 minutes you are not at Y, then you must assume that you have made a navigational error and should consider retracing your bearings to X or another obvious 'known' point before the problem becomes too great.

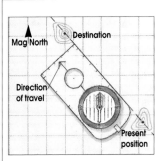

NAVIGATING WITH THE AID OF A COMPASS

A Orientating a map destination

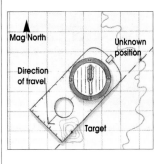

B Finding a line of travel.

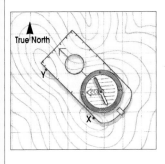

C Placing compass for map bearings

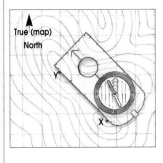

D Orientating bezel to true North

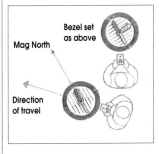

E Turn body with the compass in your hands until the needle lines up with north on the bezel

FIRST-AID AND RESCUE TECHNIQUES

The knowledge contained in this section is only a basic outline of emergency procedures. It is strongly recommended that all climbers should take a recognized first-aid course and ensure that they are fully equipped to deal with any emergency.

In any incident of trauma to a person from falls, falling rocks, or avalanches, you must check breathing, heartbeat and bleeding:

Airway – Ensure that the mouth and throat and lung passages are not blocked. If the victim is able to breathe, but is unconscious, place her in the *recovery position*; on her front/side with her head turned to one side. This enables the patient to vomit without blocking the airway. *Before moving the patient, check for obvious head, neck or back injuries.*

Breathing – If the airway is clear but the victim is not breathing, start mouth-to-mouth respiration. Continue until the patient starts to breathe, or is declared dead. *It can require many minutes of resuscitation before a severely traumatized patient can breathe without assistance. Do not give up too easily.*

Circulation – Is there a heartbeat? If not, check carefully first for major neck or back trauma, then turn the patient onto her back and start cardiopulmonary resuscitation (CPR). Continue until she is either out of trouble, or is definitely beyond help.

Dire bleeding – If the patient is bleeding profusely from open wounds, apply direct pressure via a large pad of cloth; this can be held in place by rucksack straps or similar. Smaller wounds can be ignored at this stage.

Hypothermia

This is a serious, and yet often underestimated, cause of problems in the alpine areas.

In hypothermia the internal, or core, temperature of the body starts to fall below the 37°C (98.6°F) mean. This happens because of a combination of circumstances, the most common being inadequate protective clothing for the surrounding conditions, the others being exhaustion and inadequate nutrition. The body can no longer find the energy to maintain its normal operating temperature, and starts to shut down the blood supply to extremities in order to conserve the vital organs.

In its **early stages**, hypothermia is difficult to recognize. The climber might appear more clumsy than usual, short-tempered or uncommunicative, or conversely, suddenly manic for a brief while. However, these states may not always be that different from your partner's usual behaviour and so the first stages are frequently missed!

In the **next stages** the patient is already in danger – the gait becomes stumbling, coordination goes awry, speech becomes slurred or erratic, and shivering becomes uncontrollable, then eventually stops. By now the danger zone is close – the victim

should immediately be warmed and fed energy-rich foods and drinks if possible. Rewarming often involves stopping out of the wind (a snow-hole, cave, bivvy bag or tent) and removing wet clothing, to be immediately replaced with warm, dry clothes if available, or by a warmer companion joining the victim in the sleeping bag to share body heat.

In **extreme conditions**, the body 'shuts down' completely, and the victim may become comatose or even appear to be dead. In hypothermia, the rule is: 'No-one is cold and dead, they need to be warm and dead'! Don't give up hope of recovery until rewarming has been attempted. There are numerous examples of supposedly dead hypothermia victims regaining consciousness during gradual thawing even after doctors had proclaimed them dead. Rapid evacuation followed by gradual, medically supervised thawing can revive even apparently frozen patients.

Hypothermia can usually be avoided – carry and wear suitable clothes; add clothing **as soon** as you start feeling cold; stay hydrated and eat high-energy foods. Above all, be aware of your partners – keep a 'buddy watch' going under potential hypothermia conditions. Remember that smaller, thinner people and children suffer more readily.

Helicopter rescue

In these days of compact radios and cellphones it is, in many parts of the world, relatively easy to arrange for rescue. In the European Alps and in the American alpine areas, organized and highly trained rescue teams are on 24-hour duty, with sleds, dogs, and helicopters as standard equipment. Some of this is done voluntarily and paid for by local councils or the government. In other areas, rescues must be paid for by the victim. With the increased frequency of rescues (in itself a concern to many interested parties, some of whom feel that many rescues are

POSSIBLE POINTS FOR HELICOPTER RESCUE ON A MOUNTAINSIDE

CAUTION

Hyperthermia: intensive effort in hot, dry conditions can bring about heat exhaustion or heat stroke. Even climbing in cool conditions while wearing excessive clothing can induce them.

Heat exhaustion is the less dangerous and is caused by dehydration under hot conditions. Treatment is to stop exercise, and cool the patient down; place in the shade if possible, loosen clothing, and give fluids.

Heatstroke is far more serious – it indicates the failure of the body's temperature regulation system to keep the body cool. The core temperature goes above 40°C, and the body goes into heatshock. This leads to collapse, and possibly to death if untreated. Causes and treatment are as for heat exhaustion. However, if possible the body should be sponged and fluids given intravenously.

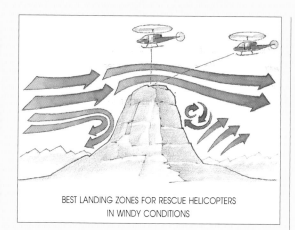

BEST LANDING ZONES FOR RESCUE HELICOPTERS
IN WINDY CONDITIONS

unnecessary and that self-rescue could have been effected, or that the often inexperienced party should never have been there in the first place), many areas are now demanding that climbers carry rescue insurance. This is highly advised, as rescue costs can amount to thousands of pounds or dollars. On the other hand, there are documented cases of climbers being hauled protesting off cliff faces screaming: 'I don't want to be rescued...', only to be told that it was for their own good!

Climbers can communicate with helicopters by using international ground symbols formed using rocks or whatever else is available. These signs should be fairly large and are as follows:

LL	All well
I	Require doctor
II	Require medical supplies
F	Require food and water
X	Unable to proceed
<—	Going this way
K	Show me which way to go
JL	Not understood
Y	Yes
N	No
V	Land here

In arm signals, one arm raised means: 'We don't need help'; both arms raised indicates the SOS signal. Other recognized aid signals are the morse code SOS (dot-dot-dot dash-dash-dash dot-dot-dot), a red flare, a white circle on a red background, and repeated flashing of a torch or mirror.

In the event of a helicopter rescue, securely tie down all loose objects (hats, ground mats, ropes, small packs and so on); keep low and do not move until ordered to do so. Remember that, on a slope, the blades of the rotor can be dangerously low on the uphill side and that the tail rotor can be spinning so fast as to be invisible. Always approach from the front, where you are visible to the pilot.

It is safest to stay hunkered down until you are called over. Remember to shield both your eyes and face, and the victim's, from flying debris.

Using a thin tape streamer or a smoke marker can help the pilot judge windspeed and direction, with a 50kph (30mph) wind being about a safe operating maximum. The greater the altitude, the less dense the air and the less manoeuvrable the helicopter will be. A landing area can be defined by three corner markers (well tied down) or by facing back to the wind and pointing with both arms in front of you. Remember, the pilot prefers to land or take off into the prevailing wind, and prefers to drop off downslope.

Allow any lowered hook or cable from the helicopter to touch ground first to discharge static before grabbing it, and do not connect it to anything until instructed.

Self-rescue

In some areas, rescue may be impossible or the injury might be so slight as to allow the party to descend to safety on its own. Useful short-distance carry techniques involve the use of a rope and a pack or ice axes to form improvized seats, while longer distances can be handled with rope-stretchers or by literally dragging the victim down snow slopes in a sitting glissade position. Further rescue techniques are discussed in the crevasse rescue section and in the rock climbing chapter.

RESCUE SIGNALS

The SOS signal

Firing off a rescue flare

We don't need help'

A broken limb is not easy to deal with halfway up a mountain. Here an improvized splint has been made from an insulated ground mattress.

Memorials erected to climbers who have died in the Nepalese Himalayas.

EXPEDITION MEDICINE

Expeditions take you far from the comforts and conveniences of society. Members of an expedition must therefore ensure that they have advanced first-aid skills and are able to deal with emergencies, including accident trauma. If there is no expedition doctor, then a number of members (if not all) should be able to administer injections and fit a drip. Doctors may argue that this is beyond the scope of the amateur; however, if you are days away from the nearest specialist, then the attempt must be made.

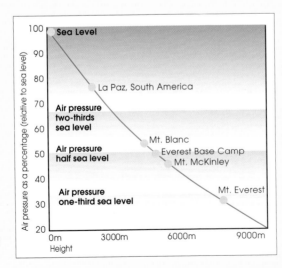

A comprehensive medical kit should be carried, including saline drips, antibiotics, antihistamines, strong analgesics, antidiarrhetics and laxatives, as well as a good supply of decongestants and cough suppressants. Expedition members will be viewed by the locals as 'medical gurus' – plenty of aspirin and brightly coloured chocolate beans will deal with most minor problems. Expeditions risk using up crucial medical supplies on the local population during the approach march, unless members are prepared to be tough.

Apart from trauma injuries and stomach conditions related to food or water contamination, the medical conditions which may occur are: heatstroke, heat exhaustion, snow-blindness, as well as various high-altitude conditions.

HIGH-ALTITUDE CONDITIONS

There are three recognized forms which may occur in conjunction with each other:

• **AMS** (acute mountain sickness) develops at increased altitudes and affects virtually everyone to a certain degree. It is character-ized by general malaise and a headache, followed by nausea, apathy, dizziness, heart palpitations, shortness of breath, and sleepiness. AMS can become incapacitating if you are not properly acclimatized.

One theory holds that anyone can acclimatize if sufficient time is taken, another that the physiological make-up of certain individuals does not allow them to acclimatize well.

Some drugs (as well as natural remedies, such as the maté tea popular with high-altitude dwellers in the Andes) seem to reduce the symptoms of AMS, possibly by allowing for better utilization of the available oxygen in the bloodstream and in the metabolic pathway. However, the best and only cure for the condition is to descend to a lower altitude, recover, and then try again. AMS can be an indicator of more serious conditions to follow and should not be ignored.

• **HAPO/E** (high-altitude pulmonary (o)edema) occurs when fluid leaks through the walls of the alveoli (air sacs) into the lungs, restricting the exchange of oxygen in the alveoli. The climber literally 'drowns' in his own fluids.

Progressive symptoms are shortness of breath, nausea, vomiting, rapid pulse (over 120 beats per minute), noisy breathing with 'crackling' sounds, cyanosis (blue colour) of lips and face, and coughing, which produces a frothy sputum eventually tinged with blood. If untreated, unconsciousness and death will follow.

Treatment involves administering oxygen, and moving the patient to a lower altitude as fast as possible.

• **HACO/E** (high-altitude cerebral (o)edema) occurs when fluid accumulates in the soft tissues of the body, particularly the brain. Symptoms start as a relentless headache of great severity, resulting from pressure build-up in the skull. Physical coordination deteriorates, progressing rapidly to slurred speech, irrationality, collapse and death. Treatment is as for HAPO.

Recovery from severe HAPO and HACO can take from several days to several weeks, so great thought should be given before reascending the mountain, even after a prolonged rest period at lower altitude.

FROSTBITE

This is literally freezing of the body tissues. The reduction of oxygen in the tissues (as a result of the high altitude) combined with the cold makes the body's extremities more susceptible to freezing. Frostbite results from an extremity losing heat faster than it can be replaced, often as a result of poor circulation, exposure to winds and/or extreme cold. As the extremity cools, so the circulation diminishes in order to preserve the core temperature of the body. This aggravates the condition, as the lack of circulation means that no energy is generated in the affected area.

Feet can freeze if wet, as the moisture conducts heat rapidly away from the skin, as well as reducing the insulating power of socks and boot shells. When water freezes it expands and forms crystals. As a result, the affected skin cells swell while the water crystals cut into the cell walls. If the frostbite has not progressed too far, the skin can be rewarmed by placing it against warm skin – a companion's abdomen or armpits – or in lukewarm water (37 to 40°C; 99 to 104°F) until the tissue is thawed.

Climbers keeping warm, in Alpamayo, Peru. Being properly dressed at all times and drinking hot fluids is the most effective way of preventing frostbite.

After thawing, frostbitten tissue should be treated as if extremely bruised, and no pressure should be placed on it for a number of days. Swaddling the area in cotton wool or soft cloth is a suitable solution. If the tissue is severely frostbitten and cannot be thoroughly thawed and then left to recover, rather leave the affected area frozen until medical help can be found or it can be properly thawed. You can walk (gingerly) on frozen feet, doing little additional damage; however, once thawed, they cannot be used for a long time without causing severe damage.

Usually frostbite can be avoided with proper clothing and proper care. Carrying spare gloves and dry socks, and checking that each team member is wearing gloves and balaclava when needed can forestall injuries. Remember that, at high altitude, you do irrational things, such as failing to wear gloves by accident or because it is just too much bother. Watch your team-mates!

CAUTION

Excessive pressure or rubbing of frozen tissue causes cells to rupture due to the sharp ice crystals. Treat frostbite injuries gently to prevent further damage. Never attempt to rewarm rapidly by means of a fire or stove.

APPENDIX FOUR – ROCK CLIMBING GRADING SYSTEMS

UIAA	FRANCE	USA	BRITAIN (TECHNICAL)	BRITAIN (SEVERITY)	AUSTRALIA	GERMANY
I	1	5.2		moderate	9	I
II	2	5.		difficult	10	II
III	3	5.4		very difficult	11	III
IV	4	5.5	4a	severe (S)	12	IV
V-					13	V
V		5.6	4b	very severe (V.S.)	14	VI
V+	5	5.7	4c		15	VIIa
VI-		5.8	5a	hard V.S.	16/17	VIIb
VI	6a	5.9		E1	18	
VI+	6a+	5.1a/b	5b		19	VIIc
VII-	6b	5.1c/d		E2	20	VIIIa
VII	6b+	5.11a	5c		21	VIIIb
VII+	6c	5.11b		E3	22	VIIIc
VIII-	6c+	5.11c	6a		23	IXa
VIII	7a/7a+	5.11d		E4	25	IXb
VIII+	7b	5.12a/b	6b		26	IXc
IX-	7b+/7c	5.12c		E5	27	Xa
IX	7c+	5.12d			28	Xb
IX+	8a	5.13a	6c		29	Xc
X-	8a+	5.13b		E6	30	
X	8b	5.13c/d	7a		31	
X+	8b+	5.14a		E7	32	
XI-	8c	5.14b	7b		33	
XI	8c+	5.14c	7c	E8/9	34	

NOTE: All grades are highly subjective. Direct comparisons from climb to climb and from grading system to grading system are bound to be both inaccurate and controversial. All grading systems are open-ended, with the current 'top' grades being (arguably) the hardest at the time of going to print.

ALPINE GRADES
Mixed (snow, ice and rock) routes in the Western Alps are given an overall grade: F – *facile* (easy); PD – *peu difficile* (moderately difficult); AD – *assez difficile* (fairly difficult); D – *difficile* (difficult); TD – *trés difficile* (very difficult); ED – *extrèmement difficile* (extremely difficult); ABO – *abominable* (abominable).

SNOW AND ICE GRADES
Conditions can vary tremendously from time to time. The Scottish system is commonly used for ice climbs. It is a I to VI scale – I is straightforward 'snow plodding' whereas VI is serious, mixed snow and rock 'technical' climbing.

AID CLIMBING
Aid routes vary from A1 to A5 (AO is used to denote simply pulling on a piece of gear). In A1, the placements are all 'bombproof' and easy to place, by A5 the placements are precarious, able to hold only body weight and with a long or even deadly potential fall if things go wrong.

BOULDERING
Bouldering grades are mostly given in the French 'Fontainebleau Power Scale': Font 6a to Font 8c; and/or the American 'Vermin' (V) Scale, from V1 to V13.

INTERNATIONAL MOUNTAINEERING ASSOCIATIONS
(CORRECT AT TIME OF PUBLICATION)

Australia
Australian Sport Climbing
Federation,
GPO Box 3786,
327 Sussex St,
Sydney NSW 2001.

Austria
Verband Alpiner Vereine
Österreichs,
Backerstrasse 16/2,
A-1010 Vienna.

Belgium
Club Alpin Belge,
rue de l'Aurore,
19 B-1050 Brussels.

Canada
Alpine Club of Canada,
PO Box 1026, Banff,
Alberta TOL OCO.

Fédération Québécoise de la
Montagne, 1415 East Jarry Street,
Montreal, Quebec.

CICE
(Commité Internationale des
Competitions des Escalades)
c/o FASI,
Via San Secondo, 92/D 10128
Torino.

Denmark
Dansk Bjiergklub,
Moelloparken 28,
Brede, DK-2800, Lyngby.

France
Fédération Française de la
Montagne et de l'Escalade,
16 rue Louis Dardenne,
F-92170 Vanves.

Germany
Deutscher Alpenverein,
Von-Kahr Strasse 2–4,
D-8099
Munich.

India
Indian Mountaineering
Foundation,
Benito Jaurez Rd,
Anand Niketan,
New Dehli 110021.

Ireland
Irish Alpine Association,
c/o AFAS, House of Sport,
Longmile Rd,
Dublin 12.

Italy
Club Alpino Italiano,
Via E. Fonseca,
Pimentel 7,
I-20127
Milano.

Federazione Arrampicata Sportiva
Italiana,
Via Saluzzo 68,
I-10125
Torino.

Japan
Japan Mountaineering Association,
Kishi Memorial Hall,
Jinnan 1-1-1 Shibuya-ku,
Tokyo 150.

Netherlands
Koninklijke Nederlandse
Alpenvereniging,
Postbus 19118,
NL-3502,
DC Utrecht.

Nederlandse Klim- en Bergsport
Bond,
Postbus 19067,
NL-3501,
DB Utrecht.

New Zealand
Alpine Club,
PO Box 3040,
Wellington.

Norway
Norges Klatreforbund,
Postboks 82, N-1351 Rud.

Norsk Tindeklub,
Postboks 8309, Hammersborg,
N-0129 Oslo 1.

South Africa
Mountain Club of South Africa,
97 Hatfield Street,
Cape Town 8001.

Switzerland
Club Alpin Suisse, Geschaftsstelle
SAC, Helvitiaplatz 4,
CH-3005 Berne.

UIAA
Postfach CH-3000
Berne 23.

United Kingdom
British Mountaineering Council,
177–179 Burton Rd,
Manchester
M20 2BB.

United States of America
American Alpine Club,
113 East 90th St,
New York,
NY 10028.

GLOSSARY

Abseil A means of descending a rope safely in a controlled fashion, the speed being controlled by friction of rope around the body or via an abseil device of some kind.

Abseil sling The sling used to hold the abseil rope. It is usually placed so as to aid retrieval of the abseil rope when pulled from below.

Accessory cord Thin rope (4 to 8mm diameter is usual) which is used for abseil slings, prusik loops and the like.

Acclimatization The progressive adaptation of the human body to the rarified air occurring at altitude.

Active camming device/unit (ACD/ACU) A spring-loaded protection device with metal cams which expand and bite harder into a rock crack or a crevice under tension (*see* SLCD).

Adze The wide, step-cutting head on an ice tool.

Aid climbing Climbing relying on the use of pegs, nuts, ACDs and other protection equipment. Also known as artificial climbing.

Alpine climbing (alpinism) Climbing which traditionally implies glacier or snow travel, higher mountains and the ascent of a peak; usually alpine ascents involve self-sufficiency of the climbers and speed in climbing.

Altimeter Barometer calibrated to read height; also used to predict weather conditions.

Altitude sickness The result of bad acclimatization, can result in death; otherwise known as AMS (acute mountain sickness).

Amphitheatre A large 'bowl' of rock, usually associated with steep rock faces.

Anchor A point of attachment of ropes or slings to rock; can be natural (rock spike or flake, or a tree) or placed (a bolt, peg, nut or similar).

Arête A narrow ridge of rock, ice or snow. On a smaller cliff, this is used to describe a steep, narrow rock ridge.

Ascender A mechanical device used to ascend a rope. Usually used in pairs (*see* jumar).

Balance move A climbing move made without a good hand-hold, where most of the adherence to the rock comes from footwork.

Bandolier Shoulder sling used to hold protection equipment during a rock climb.

Bearing The compass direction which is used to reach an objective.

Belay The 'system' used to stop a fall by means of a rope – includes the anchor, the belayer and the belay devices or method. To 'belay' is to hold the rope in such a way as to be able to arrest a fall.

Bergschrund The final big crevasse at the head of a glacier, usually where the rock wall begins or the ice face steepens.

Big wall A long, technically demanding route usually needing many days for ascent. Not every pitch need be 'climbed' by each climber; mechanical ascenders are often used by the second climber.

Bivouac To spend the night in the open while on a route or mountain. May be a 'forced bivouac' if this is unintentional.

Bolt A metal expansion bolt, glued or fastened into a predrilled hole in the rock face; used for belays or running protection.

Bombproof An anchor or running belay which is regarded as 'totally safe'.

Bouldering Unroped climbing on any small rock surface, including climbing walls and buildings.

Camming device *See* active camming device.

Carabiner (crab) Metal device which can open on one side (the gate), used to attach protection to slings or ropes or for general uses in climbing where a device that opens is needed.

CE A European standard safety marking, compulsory on new personal protective equipment.

Ceiling A large horizontal overhang.

Chickenhead Fairly large, rounded, protruding lumps of rock (usually granite) which can be used as holds or protection points.

Chimneying Climbing a fissure or 'chimney' using back- and foot-techniques against opposite walls.

Chock A nut (protection).

Chockstone Stone wedged in a crack or chimney.

Classic route A climb considered to be outstanding due to circumstances such as location, history or elegance. It can be of any climbing grade.

Committing A route or move where retreat would be difficult or impossible.

Contour A line on a map joining points of equal height above mean sea level.

Copperhead A nut with a head of malleable copper which is pounded into marginal cracks to give a point of aid.

Cornice An overhanging mass of snow on a ridge formed by wind action on newly deposited snow.

Couloir A broad gulley.

Crag A smallish outcrop of rock, usually with routes of only one or two pitches.

Crampons Metal frames with down- and front-pointing spikes, fitted to mountain boots to assist passage on hard snow or ice.

Crevasse A huge split in a glacier, frequently hidden under overlying snow cover.

Crux The most difficult part of a climb.

Deadman Shaped metal plate buried in snow as a belay anchor.

Descendeur A device used to increase friction and yet still allow the rope to move during an abseil, e.g. a figure 8 descendeur.

Dynamic belay Generally accepted belaying technique where some rope is allowed to slip through the belay system in order to reduce the forces on a climber and belay points during a fall.

Flake A thin piece of protruding rock, suitable for use as a hand-hold or to drape a sling on for protection.

Flash To ascend a route 'on sight' with no rests or falls but with the advantage of preknowledge of crucial moves.

Gear General name for climbing equipment, but usually used specifically to refer to protection equipment.

Glissade A controlled sliding descent of a snow slope, usually when standing.

Grade The 'difficulty rating' given to a climb; determined by general consensus.

Grande course A long, classic Alpine route.

Ice screw Metal screw that is hammered or screwed into the ice to give running protection or a belay anchor.

Icefall A frozen waterfall.

Jumar The original make of ascender, a metal toothed device which 'clamps' onto the rope and has since given its name to the technique of ascending ropes by means of similar ascenders.

Karabiner *See* carabiner.

Kernmantel rope Nylon or perlon rope with a 'core and sheath' construction.

Layback Method of ascending a crack or edge where the hands grip and pull while the feet provide counterforce, e.g. in a corner crack.

Marginal A runner or aid point, the ability of which to hold pressure or a fall is uncertain.

Mixed route Usually a route involving both rock and snow/ice climbing.

Natural gear Protection which is placed by the leader and removed by the second, e.g. slings, nuts, ACDs (not predrilled bolts or pegs).

Niche A small recess in a rock face.

Nose A protruding mass of rock, varying from tiny (on a crag) to huge (on a large mountain).

Nut Name for a metal wedge or chock designed to offer protection in cracks.

Objective danger Occurrences outside the control of the climber, e.g. stone fall, avalanche, lightning.

Off-width A crack too small to accommodate the body, but too large to allow for a hand or foot jam. Usually very tricky to climb.

On sight To lead a climb flawlessly the first time, with no preknowledge of the route or moves.

Open book A crack in a corner which allows for bridging with hands and feet.

Pitch A section of rock/snow/ice which is climbed between major belay points; often a pitch stops at a suitable stance or anchor point.

Piton (peg or pin) Metal spike with an attachment eye for a carabiner; hammered into crevices for use as protection.

Protection Nylon slings or metal devices (nuts, chocks, hexes, stoppers, ACDs) placed into the rock and used to prevent the climber from falling too far, and also to anchor climbers or the rope to belay points.

Prusik (prussik) Short lengths of thin cord specially tied into loops, wound around the rope in a set fashion and used as a sliding friction knot to ascend the rope.

Rack The set of protection carried on a climb.

Ramp A slab running diagonally across a face.

Rappel *See* abseil.

Redpointing A climbing style (usually only in sport climbing) where any amount and form of practice and preparation of the route is allowed providing the climb is finally led without putting any weight on the protection points.

Refuge Mountain hut.

Rock boots Lightweight, specialized, tight-fitting boots with sticky high-friction rubber soles.

Roof *See* ceiling.

Route A 'pathway' up the mountain – this can follow a recognized, written-up description or cover unknown ground, previously never ascended.

Runner The combination of protection, sling and carabiner used to stop a fall.

Second The climber who ascends the pitch after the lead climber.

Sérac A block of ice in an ice fall. Potentially hazardous as it may break off.

Skyhook Small, bent, metal hook or 'claw' used in aid climbing; sometimes even used as a runner in desperate situations.

Slab A large, often featureless, off-vertically inclined sheet of rock; best climbed with balance techniques.

Slack A climbing call for more rope.

Snap link *See* carabiner.

Solo climbing To climb alone; without a rope this is called 'free soloing'.

Spindrift Falling or blowing loose powder snow.

Spring-loaded camming device (SLCD) *See* active camming device.

Sticht plate A general term which is often used to refer to belay plates; the original was developed by Franz Sticht.

Sustained route A route with a continuous high level of difficulty.

Swaged wire A metal circlet is squeezed around the two wire ends in order to join them, making a strong, continuous loop.

Technical climbing Complex and difficult moves requiring skill, thought and technique.

Thread (Wormhole) A gap or tunnel in a rock face through which one can pass a sling for protection or even climb through if large enough.

Thrutching Inelegant, struggling climbing technique (used in awkwardly sized chimneys, etc.).

Tie on To attach the rope to the climber, usually via the harness.

Top-rope To climb a pitch without leading it; the rope is attached from above.

Topo A semi-pictorial diagram illustrating the line of a route.

Torque To twist a piece of equipment, or part of one's body, so that it sticks in a crack.

UIAA Union Internationale des Associations d'Alpinisme – the international governing body of mountaineering.

UIAGM Union Internationale des Associations des Guides de Montagne – international association of qualified mountain guides.

Via Ferrata (German: Klettersteige) Spectacular routes in the European Dolomites in particular, protected by *in situ* ladders, rails and cables.

Wall A large, steep mountain face.

Water ice Hard, brittle ice formed by the freezing of water, as opposed to snow compaction.

Wind chill The effect of wind in dissipating heat from a body; has the effect of lowering effective temperature below the actual still air temperature.

SI (Systéme Internationalé)

There has been a strong move towards the world-wide adoption of a uniform system of measurement, called metric units. SI Units are used in this book but, where other units are commonly used, both notations are included, for instance 1m (3.281ft).

INDEX

BIBLIOGRAPHY

BARTON, BOB *Outward Bound Rock Climbing Handbook*, London, WardLock 1995

BENGE, MICHAEL; RALEIGH, DUANE *Climbing Rock: Tools and Techniques*, Colorado, Elk Mountain Press 1995

BENK C.; BRAM G. *A Guide to Mountaineering Ropes*, 3rd Edition Holzer 1980

BLACK DIAMOND Catalogue, Black Diamond 1995

BLUM, ARLENE *Annapurna - A Woman's Place*, London, Granada 1984

BONINGTON, CHRIS *Quest for Adventure*, London, Hodder and Stoughton 1981

BONINGTON, CHRIS (ed) *Great Climbs*, London, Mitchell Beazley 1995

CANNING, JOHN (ed) *50 Great Journeys*, UK, Hamlyn Publishing Group 1968

CAPPON, MASSIMO *Rock and Ice Climbing*, London, Orbis Publishing Ltd. 1983

CLARKE, CHARLES *Epic Adventures: Everest*, London, Sackett and Marshall 1978

CLEARE, JOHN *Mountains*, London, MacMillan 1975

DEARDEN, PAUL *Classic Rock Climbs*, London, Blandford 1994

DMM Catalogue, DMM Wales 1997

DUMLER H.; BURKHARDT W. *The High Mountains of the Alps: 4000m Peaks*, London, Diadem Books, Seattle, The Mountaineers 1993

EDELRID *Rope Catalogue*, Allgua, Edelrid 1990

FYFFE, ALLEN; PETER, IAIN *The Handbook of Climbing*, London, Pelham Books 1990

GILLMAN, PETER (ed) *Everest - the Best Writing and Pictures from Seventy Years of Human Endeavour*, London, Peter Gillman Ltd. 1993

GODDARD, DALE; NEUMANN, UDO *Performance Rock Climbing*, Mechanicsburg, Stackpole Books 1993

GREENBANK, ANTHONY *Climbing for Young People*, London, Harrap 1977

HERZOG, MAURICE *Annapurna: Conquest of the First 8000m Peak*, Oxford, Alden Press 1953

HORNBEIN, THOMAS *Everest, the West Ridge*, London, George Allen & Unwin 1971

JOHNSTON, TURLOUGH *Rock Climbers' Manual*, London, Blandford 1995

KEAY, WALLY *Land Navigation*, Rugby, Belgrave Frost 1989

LYE, KEITH *Our World, The Earth*, London, Hamlyn 1991

MESSNER, REINHOLD *The Big Walls*, London, Kaye and Ward 1978

MESSNER, REINHOLD *K2, Mountain of Mountains*, London, Kaye and Ward 1981

MILES J.; PRIEST S. *Adventure Education*, USA, Venture Publishing 1990

MOUNTAINEERS, THE *Mountaineering, The Freedom of the Hills*, 5th Edition, Washington, The Mountaineers 1992

PERRIN, JIM (ed) *Mirrors in the Cliffs*, London, Diadem 1983

RÉBUFFAT, GASTON *The Mont Blanc Massif, the 100 Finest Routes*, London, Kaye and Ward 1975

SCOTT, DOUG *Himalayan Climber*, London, Diadem Books 1992

SHIPTON, ERIC *Blank on the Map*, London, Hodder and Stoughton 1938

TASKER, JOE *Everest the Cruel Way*, London, Eyre Methuen 1981

UNSWORTH, WALT *Encyclopaedia of Mountaineering*, London, Hodder and Stoughton 1992

UNSWORTH, WALT *This Climbing Game*, London, Penguin 1985

VAN EEDEN, JOHAN *The South African Mountain Leadership Guide*, Cape Town, National Book Printers 1991

VON KANEL, JURG *Schweiz Plaisir*, Reichenbach, Filidor 1992

WALKER, KEVIN *Learn Rock Climbing in a Weekend*, London, Dorling Kindersley 1996

PUBLISHER'S ACKNOWLEDGEMENTS

The publisher would like to thank Simon Larsen of Ram Mountaineering (agents for Black Diamond Equipment and New England Ropes), and Geoff, Jeanne and Derek Ward of Outward Ventures (agents for DMM, Wild Country, Marlow Ropes, LaSportiva and MSR), for their unstinting help, good humour and generosity in providing equipment for photographic shoots. In addition, the publisher would like to thank Jeanne O'Brien of Black Diamond Equipment and Paul Simkiss from DMM for their assistance with picture sourcing. A final word of thanks goes to all the climbers who have given of their time and knowledge, particularly Maarten Turkstra and Leonard Rust.

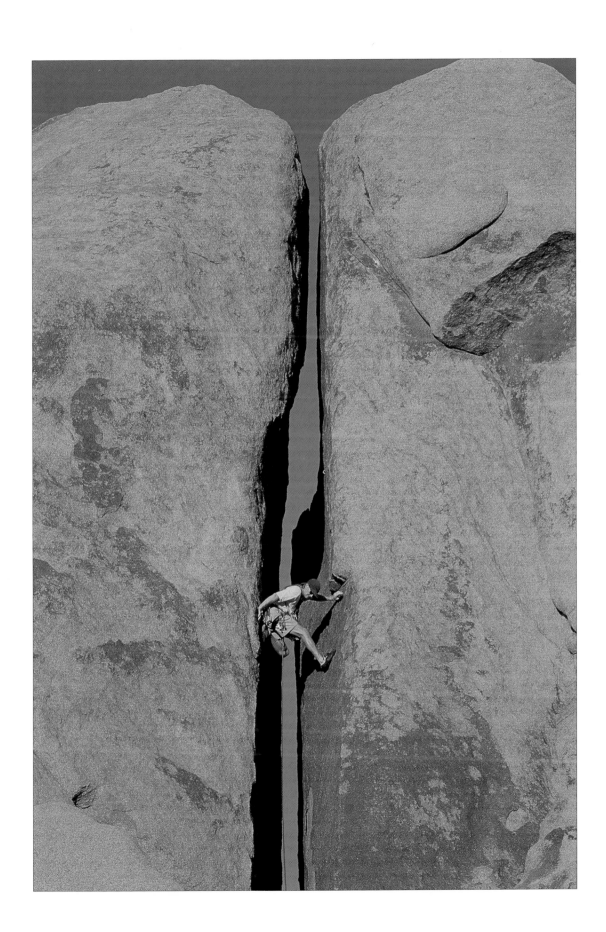